An Essay on Liberation

An Essay on Liberation

BY HERBERT MARCUSE

BEACON PRESS : BOSTON

Acknowledgments

T HANKS AGAIN to my friends who read the manuscript and whose comments and criticism I heeded throughout: especially Leo Lowenthal (University of California at Berkeley), Arno J. Mayer (Princeton University), and Barrington Moore, Jr. (Harvard University). My wife discussed with me every part and problem of the manuscript. Without her cooperation, this essay would have appeared much sooner. I am grateful to her that it didn't.

Preface

T HE GROWING OPPOSITION to the global dominion of corporate capitalism is confronted by the sustained power of this dominion: its economic and military hold in the four continents, its neocolonial empire, and, most important, its unshaken capacity to subject the majority of the underlying population to its overwhelming productivity and force. This global power keeps the socialist orbit on the defensive, all too costly not only in terms of military expenditures but also in the perpetuation of a repressive bureaucracy. The development of socialism thus continues to be deflected from its original goals, and the competitive coexistence with the West generates values and aspirations for which the American standard of living serves as a model.

Now, however, this threatening homogeneity has been loosening up, and an alternative is beginning to break into the repressive continuum. This alternative is not so much a different road to socialism as an emergence of different goals and values, different aspirations in the men and women who resist and deny the massive exploitative power of corporate capitalism even in its most comfortable and liberal realizations. The Great Refusal takes a variety of forms.

In Vietnam, in Cuba, in China, a revolution is being defended and driven forward which struggles to eschew the bureaucratic administration of socialism. The guerrilla forces in Latin America seem to be animated by that same subversive impulse: liberation. At the same time, the apparently impregnable economic fortress of corporate capitalism shows signs of mounting strain: it seems that even the United States cannot indefinitely deliver its goods — guns and butter, napalm and color TV. The ghetto populations may well become the first mass basis of revolt (though not of revolution). The student opposition is spreading in the old socialist as well as capitalist countries. In France, it has for the first time challenged the full force of the regime and recaptured, for a short moment, the libertarian power of the red and the black flags; moreover, it has demonstrated the prospects for an enlarged basis. The temporary suppression of the rebellion will not reverse the trend.

None of these forces *is* the alternative. However, they outline, in very different dimensions, the limits of the established societies, of their power of containment. When these limits are reached, the Establishment may initiate a new order of totalitarian suppression. But beyond these limits, there is also the space, both physical and mental, for building a realm of freedom which is not that of the present: liberation also from the liberties of exploitative order — a liberation which must precede the construction of a free society, one which necessitates an historical break with the past and the present.

It would be irresponsible to overrate the present chances of these forces (this essay will stress the obstacles and "delays"), but the facts are there, facts which are not only the symbols but also the embodiments of hope. They confront the critical theory of society with the task of reexamining the prospects for the emergence of a socialist society qualitatively different from existing societies, the task of redefining socialism and its preconditions.

In the following chapters, I attempt to develop some ideas first submitted in *Eros and Civilization* and in *One-Dimensional Man,* then further discussed in "Repressive Tolerance" and in lectures delivered in recent years, mostly to student audiences in the United States and in Europe. This essay was written before the events of May and June 1968 in France. I have merely added some footnotes in the way of documentation. The coincidence between some of the ideas suggested in my essay, and those formulated by the young militants was to me striking. The radical utopian character of their demands far surpasses the hypotheses of my essay; and yet, these demands were developed and formulated in the course of action itself; they are expressions of concrete political practice. The militants have invalidated the concept of "utopia" — they have denounced a vicious ideology. No matter whether their action was a revolt or an abortive revolution, it is a turning point. In proclaiming the "permanent challenge" (*la contestation permanente*), the "permanent education," the Great Refusal, they recognize the mark of social repression, even in the most sublime manifestations of traditional culture, even in the most spectacular manifestations of technical progress. They have again raised a specter (and this time a specter which haunts not only the bourgeoisie but all exploitative bureaucracies): the specter of a revolution which subordinates the development of productive forces and higher standards of living to the requirements of creating solidarity for the human species, for abolishing poverty and misery beyond all national frontiers and spheres of interest, for the attainment of peace. In one word: they have taken the idea of revolution out of the continuum of repression and placed it into its authentic dimension: that of liberation.

The young militants know or sense that what is at stake is simply their life, the life of human beings which has become a plaything in the hands of politicians and managers and generals. The rebels want to take it out of these hands and make it worth living; they realize that this is still possible today, and that the attainment of this goal necessitates a struggle which can no longer be contained by the rules and regulations of a pseudo-democracy in a Free Orwellian World. To them I dedicate this essay.

An Essay on Liberation

Introduction

U P TO NOW, it has been one of the principal tenets of the critical theory of society (and particularly Marxian theory) to refrain from what might be reasonably called utopian speculation. Social theory is supposed to analyze existing societies in the light of their own functions and capabilities and to identify demonstrable tendencies (if any) which might lead beyond the existing state of affairs. By logical inference from the prevailing conditions and institutions, critical theory may also be able to determine the basic institutional changes which are the prerequisites for the transition to a higher stage of development: "higher" in the sense of a more rational and equitable use of resources, minimization of destructive conflicts, and enlargement of the realm of freedom. But beyond these limits, critical theory did not venture for fear of losing its scientific character.

I believe that this restrictive conception must be revised, and that the revision is suggested, and even necessitated, by the actual evolution of contemporary societies. The dynamic of their productivity deprives "utopia" of its traditional unreal content: what is denounced as "utopian" is no longer that which has "no place" and cannot have any place in the historical universe, but rather that which is blocked from coming about by the power of the established societies.

Utopian possibilities are inherent in the technical and technological forces of advanced capitalism and socialism: the rational utilization of these forces on a global scale would terminate poverty and scarcity within a very foreseeable future. But we know now that neither their rational use nor — and this is decisive — their collective control by the "immediate producers" (the workers) would by itself eliminate domination and exploitation: a bureaucratic welfare state would still be a state of repression which would continue even into the "second phase of socialism," when each is to receive "according to his needs."

What is now at stake are the needs themselves. At this stage, the question is no longer: how can the individual satisfy his own needs without hurting others, but rather: how can he satisfy his needs without hurting himself, without reproducing, through his aspirations and satisfactions, his dependence on an exploitative apparatus which, in satisfying his needs, perpetuates his servitude? The advent of a free society would be characterized by the fact that the growth of well-being turns into an essentially new quality of life. This qualitative change must occur in the needs, in the infrastructure of man (itself a dimension of the infrastructure of society): the new direction, the new institutions and relationships of production, must express the ascent of needs and satisfactions very different from and even antagonistic to those prevalent in the exploitative societies. Such a change would constitute the instinctual basis for freedom which the long history of class society has blocked. Freedom would become the environment of an organism which is no longer capable of adapting to the

competitive performances required for well-being under
domination, no longer capable of tolerating the aggressiveness, brutality, and ugliness of the established way of life.
The rebellion would then have taken root in the very nature, the "biology" of the individual; and on these new
grounds, the rebels would redefine the objectives and the
strategy of the political struggle, in which alone the concrete goals of liberation can be determined.

Is such a change in the "nature" of man conceivable? I
believe so, because technical progress has reached a stage
in which reality no longer need be defined by the debilitating competition for social survival and advancement. The
more these technical capacities outgrow the framework of
exploitation within which they continue to be confined and
abused, the more they propel the drives and aspirations of
men to a point at which the necessities of life cease to demand the aggressive performances of "earning a living,"
and the "non-necessary" becomes a vital need. This
proposition, which is central in Marxian theory, is familiar
enough, and the managers and publicists of corporate capitalism are well aware of its meaning; they are prepared to
"contain" its dangerous consequences. The radical opposition also is aware of these prospects, but the critical
theory which is to guide political practice still lags behind.
Marx and Engels refrained from developing concrete concepts of the possible forms of freedom in a socialist society;
today, such restraint no longer seems justified. The growth
of the productive forces suggests possibilities of human
liberty very different from, and beyond those envisaged
at the earlier stage. Moreover, these real possibilities suggest that the gap which separates a free society from
the existing societies would be wider and deeper precisely
to the degree to which the repressive power and produc-

tivity of the latter shape man and his environment in their image and interest.

For the world of human freedom cannot be built by the established societies, no matter how much they may streamline and rationalize their dominion. Their class structure, and the perfected controls required to sustain it, generate needs, satisfactions, and values which reproduce the servitude of the human existence. This "voluntary" servitude (voluntary inasmuch as it is introjected into the individuals), which justifies the benevolent masters, can be broken only through a political practice which reaches the roots of containment and contentment in the infrastructure of man, a political practice of methodical disengagement from and refusal of the Establishment, aiming at a radical transvaluation of values. Such a practice involves a break with the familiar, the routine ways of seeing, hearing, feeling, understanding things so that the organism may become receptive to the potential forms of a nonaggressive, nonexploitative world.

No matter how remote from these notions the rebellion may be, no matter how destructive and self-destructive it may appear, no matter how great the distance between the middle-class revolt in the metropoles and the life-and-death struggle of the wretched of the earth — common to them is the depth of the Refusal. It makes them reject the rules of the game that is rigged against them, the ancient strategy of patience and persuasion, the reliance on the Good Will in the Establishment, its false and immoral comforts, its cruel affluence.

I. A Biological Foundation
for Socialism?

In the affluent society, capitalism comes into its own. The two mainsprings of its dynamic — the escalation of commodity production and productive exploitation — join and permeate all dimensions of private and public existence. The available material and intellectual resources (the potential of liberation) have so much outgrown the established institutions that only the systematic increase in waste, destruction, and management keeps the system going. The opposition which escapes suppression by the police, the courts, the representatives of the people, and the people themselves, finds expression in the diffused rebellion among the youth and the intelligentsia, and in the daily struggle of the persecuted minorities. The armed class struggle is waged outside: by the wretched of the earth who fight the affluent monster.

The critical analysis of this society calls for new categories: moral, political, aesthetic. I shall try to develop them in the course of the discussion. The category of obscenity will serve as an introduction.

This society is obscene in producing and indecently exposing a stifling abundance of wares while depriving its victims abroad of the necessities of life; obscene in stuffing itself and its garbage cans while poisoning and burning the scarce foodstuffs in the fields of its aggression; obscene in the words and smiles of its politicians and entertainers; in its prayers, in its ignorance, and in the wisdom of its kept intellectuals.

Obscenity is a moral concept in the verbal arsenal of the Establishment, which abuses the term by applying it, not to expressions of its own morality but to those of another. Obscene is not the picture of a naked woman who exposes her pubic hair but that of a fully clad general who exposes his medals rewarded in a war of aggression; obscene is not the ritual of the Hippies but the declaration of a high dignitary of the Church that war is necessary for peace. Linguistic therapy — that is, the effort to free words (and thereby concepts) from the all but total distortion of their meanings by the Establishment — demands the transfer of moral standards (and of their validation) from the Establishment to the revolt against it. Similarly, the sociological and political vocabulary must be radically reshaped: it must be stripped of its false neutrality; it must be methodically and provocatively "moralized" in terms of the Refusal. Morality is not necessarily and not primarily ideological. In the face of an amoral society, it becomes a political weapon, an effective force which drives people to burn their draft cards, to ridicule national leaders, to demonstrate in the streets, and to unfold signs saying, "Thou shalt not kill," in the nation's churches.

The reaction to obscenity is shame, usually interpreted as the physiological manifestation of the sense of guilt accompanying the transgression of a taboo. The obscene exposures of the affluent society normally provoke neither shame nor a sense of guilt, although this society violates some of the most fundamental moral taboos of civilization.

The term obscenity belongs to the sexual sphere; shame and the sense of guilt arise in the Oedipal situation. If in this respect social morality is rooted in sexual morality, then the shamelessness of the affluent society and its effective repression of the sense of guilt would indicate a decline of shame and guilt feeling in the sexual sphere. And indeed, the exposure of the (for all practical purposes) naked body is permitted and even encouraged, and the taboos on pre- and extramarital intercourse are considerably relaxed. Thus we are faced with the contradiction that the liberalization of sexuality provides an instinctual basis for the repressive and aggressive power of the affluent society.

This contradiction can be resolved if we understand that the liberalization of the Establishment's own morality takes place within the framework of effective controls; kept within this framework, the liberalization strengthens the cohesion of the whole. The relaxation of taboos alleviates the sense of guilt and binds (though with considerable ambivalence) the "free" individuals libidinally to the institutionalized fathers. They are powerful but also tolerant fathers, whose management of the nation and its economy delivers and protects the liberties of the citizens. On the other hand, if the violation of taboos transcends the sexual sphere and leads to refusal and rebellion, the sense of guilt is not alleviated and repressed but rather transferred: not we, but the fathers, are guilty; they are not tolerant but false; they want to redeem their own guilt by making us, the sons, guilty; they have created a world of hypocrisy and violence in which we do not wish to live. Instinctual revolt turns into political rebellion, and against this union, the Establishment mobilizes its full force.

This union provokes such a response because it reveals the prospective scope of social change at this stage of de-

velopment, the extent to which the radical political practice
involves a cultural subversion. The refusal with which the
opposition confronts the existing society is affirmative in
that it envisages a new culture which fulfills the humanistic
promises betrayed by the old culture. Political radicalism
thus implies moral radicalism: the emergence of a morality
which might precondition man for freedom. This radicalism
activates the elementary, organic foundation of morality in
the human being. Prior to all ethical behavior in accordance
with specific social standards, prior to all ideological expression, morality is a "disposition" of the organism, perhaps rooted in the erotic drive to counter aggressiveness,
to create and preserve "ever greater unities" of life. We
would then have, this side of all "values," an instinctual
foundation for solidarity among human beings — a solidarity which has been effectively repressed in line with the
requirements of class society but which now appears as a
precondition for liberation.

To the degree to which this foundation is itself historical
and the malleability of "human nature" reaches into the
depth of man's instinctual structure, changes in morality
may "sink down" into the "biological"[1] dimension and

---

[1] I use the terms "biological" and "biology" not in the sense of the scientific discipline, but in order to designate the process and the dimension
in which inclinations, behavior patterns, and aspirations become vital
needs which, if not satisfied, would cause dysfunction of the organism.
Conversely, socially induced needs and aspirations may result in a more
pleasurable organic behavior. If biological needs are defined as those
which must be satisfied and for which no adequate substitute can be
provided, certain cultural needs can "sink down" into the biology of man.
We could then speak, for example, of the biological need of freedom, or
of some aesthetic needs as having taken root in the organic structure of
man, in his "nature," or rather "second nature." This usage of the term
"biological" does not imply or assume anything as to the way in which
needs are physiologically expressed and transmitted.

modify organic behavior. Once a specific morality is firmly established as a norm of social behavior, it is not only intro- jected — it also operates as a norm of "organic" behavior: the organism receives and reacts to certain stimuli and "ig- nores" and repels others in accord with the introjected morality, which is thus promoting or impeding the function of the organism as a living cell in the respective society. In this way, a society constantly re-creates, this side of con- sciousness and ideology, patterns of behavior and aspira- tion as part of the "nature" of its people, and unless the re- volt reaches into this "second" nature, into these ingrown patterns, social change will remain "incomplete," even self- defeating.

The so-called consumer economy and the politics of cor- porate capitalism have created a second nature of man which ties him libidinally and aggressively to the commod- ity form. The need for possessing, consuming, handling, and constantly renewing the gadgets, devices, instruments, engines, offered to and imposed upon the people, for using these wares even at the danger of one's own destruction, has become a "biological" need in the sense just defined. The second nature of man thus militates against any change that would disrupt and perhaps even abolish this depend- ence of man on a market ever more densely filled with merchandise — abolish his existence as a consumer con- suming himself in buying and selling. The needs generated by this system are thus eminently stabilizing, conservative needs: the counterrevolution anchored in the instinctual structure.

The market has always been one of exploitation and thereby of domination, insuring the class structure of so- ciety. However, the productive process of advanced capi- talism has altered the form of domination: the technological veil covers the brute presence and the operation of the class interest in the merchandise. Is it still necessary to state that not technology, not technique, not the machine are the engines of repression, but the presence, in them, of the masters who determine their number, their life span, their power, their place in life, and the need for them? Is it still necessary to repeat that science and technology are the great vehicles of liberation, and that it is only their use and restriction in the repressive society which makes them into vehicles of domination?

Not the automobile is repressive, not the television set is repressive, not the household gadgets are repressive, but the automobile, the television, the gadgets which, produced in accordance with the requirements of profitable exchange, have become part and parcel of the people's own existence, own "actualization." Thus they have to buy part and parcel of their own existence on the market; this existence is the realization of capital. The naked class interest builds the unsafe and obsolescent automobiles, and through them promotes destructive energy; the class interest employs the mass media for the advertising of violence and stupidity, for the creation of captive audiences. In doing so, the masters only obey the demand of the public, of the masses; the famous law of supply and demand establishes the harmony between the rulers and the ruled. This harmony is indeed preestablished to the degree to which the masters have created the public which asks for their wares, and asks for them more insistently if it can release, in and through the wares, its frustration and the aggressiveness resulting from this frustration. Self-determination, the autonomy of the individual, asserts itself in the right to race his automobile, to handle his power tools, to buy a gun, to communicate to mass audiences his opinion, no matter how ignorant, how aggressive, it may be. Organized capitalism has sublimated and turned to socially productive use frustration and primary aggressiveness on an unprecedented scale — unprecedented not in terms of the quantity of violence but rather in terms of its capacity to produce long-range contentment and satisfaction, to reproduce the "voluntary servitude." To be sure, frustration, unhappiness, and sickness remain the basis of this sublimation, but the productivity and the brute power of the system still keep the basis well under control. The achievements justify the system of domination. The established values become the people's own values: adaptation turns into spontaneity, autonomy; and the choice between social necessities appears as freedom. In this sense, the continuing exploitation is not only hidden behind the technological veil, but actually "transfigured." The capitalist production relations are responsible not only for the servitude and toil but also for the greater happiness and fun available to the majority of the population — and they deliver more goods than before.

Neither its vastly increased capacity to produce the commodities of satisfaction nor the peaceful management of class conflicts rendered possible by this capacity cancels the essential features of capitalism, namely, the private appropriation of surplus value (steered but not abolished by government intervention) and its realization in the corporate interest. Capitalism reproduces itself by transforming itself, and this transformation is mainly in the improvement of exploitation. Do exploitation and domination cease to be what they are and what they do to man if they are no longer suffered, if they are "compensated" by previously unknown comforts? Does labor cease to be debilitating if mental energy increasingly replaces physical energy in producing the goods and services which sustain a system that makes hell of large areas of the globe? An affirmative answer would justify any form of oppression which keeps the populace calm and content; while a negative answer would deprive the individual of being the judge of his own happiness.

The notion that happiness is an objective condition which demands more than subjective feelings has been effectively obscured; its validity depends on the real solidarity of the species "man," which a society divided into antagonistic classes and nations cannot achieve. As long as this is the history of mankind, the "state of nature," no matter how refined, prevails: a civilized *bellum omnium contra omnes*, in which the happiness of the ones must coexist with the suffering of the others. The First International was the last attempt to realize the solidarity of the species by grounding it in that social class in which the subjective and objective interest, the particular and the universal, coincided (the International is the late concretization of the abstract philosophical concept of "man as man," human being, *"Gattungswesen,"* which plays such a decisive role in Marx' and Engels' early writings). Then, the Spanish civil war aroused this solidarity, which is the driving power of liberation, in the unforgettable, hopeless fight of a tiny minority against the combined forces of fascist and liberal capitalism. Here, in the international brigades which, with their poor weapons, withstood overwhelming technical superiority, was the union of young intellectuals and workers — the union which has become the desperate goal of today's radical opposition.

Attainment of this goal is thwarted by the integration of the organized (and not only the organized) laboring class into the system of advanced capitalism. Under its impact, the distinction between the real and the immediate interest of the exploited has collapsed. This distinction, far from being an abstract idea, was guiding the strategy of the Marxist movements; it expressed the necessity transcending the economic struggle of the laboring classes, to extend wage demands and demands for the improvement of working conditions to the political arena, to drive the class struggle to the point at which the system itself would be at stake, to make foreign as well as domestic policy, the national as well as the class interest, the target of this struggle. The real interest, the attainment of conditions in which man could shape his own life, was that of no longer subordinating his life to the requirements of profitable production, to an apparatus controlled by forces beyond his control. And the attainment of such conditions meant the abolition of capitalism.

It is not simply the higher standard of living, the illusory bridging of the consumer gap between the rulers and the ruled, which has obscured the distinction between the real and the immediate interest of the ruled. Marxian theory soon recognized that impoverishment does not necessarily provide the soil for revolution, that a highly developed consciousness and imagination may generate a vital need for radical change in advanced material conditions. The power of corporate capitalism has stifled the emergence of such a consciousness and imagination; its mass media have adjusted the rational and emotional faculties to its market and its policies and steered them to defense of its dominion. The narrowing of the consumption gap has rendered possible the mental and instinctual coordination of the laboring classes: the majority of organized labor shares the stabilizing, counterrevolutionary needs of the middle classes, as evidenced by their behavior as consumers of the material and cultural merchandise, by their emotional revulsion

against the nonconformist intelligentsia. Conversely, where
the consumer gap is still wide, where the capitalist culture
has not yet reached into every house or hut, the system of
stabilizing needs has its limits; the glaring contrast between the privileged class and the exploited leads to a
radicalization of the underprivileged. This is the case of
the ghetto population and the unemployed in the United
States; this is also the case of the laboring classes in the
more backward capitalist countries.[2]

By virtue of its basic position in the production process,
by virtue of its numerical weight and the weight of exploitation, the working class is still the historical agent of revolution; by virtue of its sharing the stabilizing needs of the
system, it has become a conservative, even counterrevolutionary force. Objectively, "in-itself," labor still is the potentially revolutionary class; subjectively, "for-itself," it is
not. This theoretical conception has concrete significance in
the prevailing situation, in which the working class may
help to circumscribe the scope and the targets of political
practice.

In the advanced capitalist countries, the radicalization
of the working classes is counteracted by a socially engineered arrest of consciousness, and by the development and
satisfaction of needs which perpetuate the servitude of the
exploited. A vested interest in the existing system is thus
fostered in the instinctual structure of the exploited, and
the rupture with the continuum of repression — a necessary precondition of liberation — does not occur. It follows
that the radical change which is to transform the existing
society into a free society must reach into a dimension of
the human existence hardly considered in Marxian theory
— the "biological" dimension in which the vital, imperative

[2] See pp. 53 f. below for further discussion.

needs and satisfactions of man assert themselves. Inasmuch as these needs and satisfactions reproduce a life in servitude, liberation presupposes changes in this biological dimension, that is to say, different instinctual needs, different reactions of the body as well as the mind.

The qualitative difference between the existing societies and a free society affects all needs and satisfactions beyond the animal level, that is to say, all those which are essential to the *human* species, man as rational animal. All these needs and satisfactions are permeated with the exigencies of profit and exploitation. The entire realm of competitive performances and standardized fun, all the symbols of status, prestige, power, of advertised virility and charm, of commercialized beauty — this entire realm kills in its citizens the very disposition, the organs, for the alternative: freedom without exploitation.

Triumph and end of introjection: the stage where the people cannot reject the system of domination without rejecting themselves, their own repressive instinctual needs and values. We would have to conclude that liberation would mean subversion against the will and against the prevailing interests of the great majority of the people. In this false identification of social and individual needs, in this deep-rooted, "organic" adaptation of the people to a terrible but profitably functioning society, lie the limits of democratic persuasion and evolution. On the overcoming of these limits depends the establishment of democracy.[3]

It is precisely this excessive adaptability of the human organism which propels the perpetuation and extension of the commodity form and, with it, the perpetuation and extension of the social controls over behavior and satisfaction.

[3] For further discussion see pp. 64 f. below.

The ever-increasing complexity of the social structure will make some form of regimentation unavoidable, freedom and privacy may come to constitute antisocial luxuries and their attainment to involve real hardships. In consequence, there may emerge by selection a stock of human beings suited genetically to accept as a matter of course a regimented and sheltered way of life in a teeming and polluted world, from which all wilderness and fantasy of nature will have disappeared. The domesticated farm animal and the laboratory rodent on a controlled regimen in a controlled environment will then become true models for the study of man.

Thus, it is apparent that food, natural resources, supplies of power, and other elements involved in the operation of the body machine and of the individual establishment are not the only factors to be considered in determining the optimum number of people that can live on earth. Just as important for maintaining the *human qualities* of life is an environment in which it is possible to satisfy the longing for quiet, privacy, independence, initiative, and some open space. . . .[4]

Capitalist progress thus not only reduces the environment of freedom, the "open space" of the human existence, but also the "longing," the need for such an environment. And in doing so, quantitative progress militates against qualitative change even if the institutional barriers against radical education and action are surmounted. This is the vicious circle: the rupture with the self-propelling conservative continuum of needs must *precede* the revolution which is to usher in a free society, but such rupture itself can be envisaged only in a revolution — a revolution which would be driven by the vital need to be freed from the admin-

[4] René Dubos, *Man Adapting* (New Haven and London: Yale University Press, 1965), pp. 313–314.

istered comforts and the destructive productivity of the exploitative society, freed from smooth heteronomy, a revolution which, by virtue of this "biological" foundation, would have the chance of turning quantitative technical progress into qualitatively different ways of life — precisely because it would be a revolution occurring at a high level of material and intellectual development, one which would enable man to conquer scarcity and poverty. If this idea of a radical transformation is to be more than idle speculation, it must have an objective foundation in the production process of advanced industrial society,[5] in its technical capabilities and their use.

For freedom indeed depends largely on technical progress, on the advancement of science. But this fact easily obscures the essential precondition: in order to become vehicles of freedom, science and technology would have to change their present direction and goals; they would have to be reconstructed in accord with a new sensibility — the demands of the life instincts. Then one could speak of a technology of liberation, product of a scientific imagination free to project and design the forms of a human universe without exploitation and toil. But this *gaya scienza* is conceivable only after the historical break in the continuum of domination — as expressive of the needs of a new type of man.[6]

---

[5] I shall discuss the existence of such a foundation in Chapter III.

[6] The critique of the prevailing scientific establishment as ideological, and the idea of a science which has really come into its own, was expressed in a manifesto issued by the militant students of Paris in May 1968 as follows:

"Refusons aussi la division de la *science* et de *l'idéologie*, la plus pernicieuse de toutes puisqu'elle est sécrétée par nous-mêmes. Nous ne voulons pas plus être gouvernés passivement par les lois de la *science* que par celle de l'économie ou les *impératifs* de la technique. La science est un

The idea of a new type of man as the member (though not as the builder) of a socialist society appears in Marx and Engels in the concept of the "all-round individual," free to engage in the most varying activities. In the socialist society corresponding to this idea, the free development of individual faculties would replace the subjection of the individual to the division of labor. But no matter what activities the all-round individual would choose, they would be activities which are bound to lose the quality of freedom if exercised "en masse" — and they would be "en masse," for even the most authentic socialist society would inherit the population growth and the mass basis of advanced capitalism. The early Marxian example of the free individuals alternating between hunting, fishing, criticizing, and so on, had a joking-ironical sound from the beginning, indicative of the impossibility anticipating the ways in which liberated human beings would use their freedom. However, the embarrassingly ridiculous sound may also indicate the degree to which this vision has become obsolete and pertains to a stage of the development of the productive forces which has been surpassed. The later Marxian concept implies the continued separation between the realm of necessity and the realm of freedom, between labor and leisure — not only in time, but also in such a manner that the same subject lives a different life in the two realms. According to this Marxian conception, the realm of necessity would con-

---

art dont l'originalité est d'avoir des applications possibles hors d'elle-même.

"Elle ne peut cependant être normative que pour elle-même. Refusons son impérialisme mystifiant, caution de tous les abus et reculs, y compris en son sein, et remplaçons-le par un choix réel parmi les possibles qu'elle nous offre" (*Quelle Université? Quelle Société?* Textes réunis par le centre de regroupement des informations universitaires. Paris: Editions du Seuil, 1968, p. 148).

tinue under socialism to such an extent that real human freedom would prevail only outside the entire sphere of socially necessary labor. Marx rejects the idea that work can ever become play.[7] Alienation would be reduced with the progressive reduction of the working day, but the latter would remain a day of unfreedom, rational but not free. However, the development of the productive forces beyond their capitalist organization suggests the possibility of freedom *within* the realm of necessity. The quantitative reduction of necessary labor could turn into quality (freedom), not in proportion to the reduction but rather to the transformation of the working day, a transformation in which the stupefying, enervating, pseudo-automatic jobs of capitalist progress would be abolished. But the construction of such a society presupposes a type of man with a different sensitivity as well as consciousness: men who would speak a different language, have different gestures, follow different impulses; men who have developed an instinctual barrier against cruelty, brutality, ugliness. Such an instinctual transformation is conceivable as a factor of social change only if it enters the social division of labor, the production relations themselves. They would be shaped by men and women who have the good conscience of being human, tender, sensuous, who are no longer ashamed of themselves — for "the token of freedom attained, that is, no longer being ashamed of ourselves" (Nietzsche, *Die Fröhliche Wissenschaft*, Book III, 275). The imagination of such men and women would fashion their reason and tend to make the process of production a process of creation. This is the utopian concept of socialism which envisages the ingression

[7] For a far more "utopian" conception see the by now familiar passage in the *Grundrisse der Kritik der Politischen Oekonomie* (Berlin: Dietz, 1953), pp. 596 ff., and p. 49 below.

of freedom into the realm of necessity, and the union between causality by necessity and causality by freedom.
The first would mean passing from Marx to Fourier; the
second from realism to surrealism.[8]

A utopian conception? It has been the great, real, transcending force, the *"idée neuve,"* in the first powerful rebellion against the whole of the existing society, the rebellion
for the total transvaluation of values, for qualitatively different ways of life: the May rebellion in France. The graffiti
of the *"jeunesse en colère"* joined Karl Marx and André
Breton; the slogan *"l'imagination au pouvoir"* went well
with *"les comités (soviets) partout";* the piano with the jazz
player stood well between the barricades; the red flag well
fitted the statue of the author of *Les Misérables;* and striking students in Toulouse demanded the revival of the language of the Troubadours, the Albigensians. The new sensibility has become a political force. It crosses the frontier
between the capitalist and the communist orbit; it is contagious because the atmosphere, the climate of the established societies, carries the virus.

[8] See p. 31 below.

II. The New Sensibility

THE NEW SENSIBILITY has become a political factor. This event, which may well indicate a turning point in the evolution of contemporary societies, demands that critical theory incorporate the new dimension into its concepts, project its implications for the possible construction of a free society. Such a society presupposes throughout the achievements of the existing societies, especially their scientific and technical achievements. Released from their service in the cause of exploitation, they could be mobilized for the global elimination of poverty and toil. True, this redirection of the intellectual and material production already presupposes the revolution in the capitalist world; the theoretical projection seems to be fatally premature — were it not for the fact that the awareness of the transcendent possibilities of freedom must become a driving power in the consciousness and the imagination which prepare the soil for this revolution. The latter will be essentially different, and effective, precisely to the degree to which it is carried forward by this power.

The new sensibility, which expresses the ascent of the life instincts over aggressiveness and guilt, would foster, on a social scale, the vital need for the abolition of injustice and misery and would shape the further evolution of the "standard of living." The life instincts would find rational expression (sublimation) in planning the distribution of the socially necessary labor time within and among the various branches of production, thus setting priorities of goals and choices: not only what to produce but also the "form" of the product. The liberated consciousness would promote the development of a science and technology free to discover and realize the possibilities of things and men in the protection and gratification of life, playing with the potentialities of form and matter for the attainment of this goal. Technique would then tend to become art, and art would tend to form reality: the opposition between imagination and reason, higher and lower faculties, poetic and scientific thought, would be invalidated. Emergence of a new Reality Principle: under which a new sensibility and a desublimated scientific intelligence would combine in the creation of an *aesthetic ethos.*

The term "aesthetic," in its dual connotation of "pertaining to the senses" and "pertaining to art," may serve to designate the quality of the productive-creative process in an environment of freedom. Technique, assuming the features of art, would translate subjective sensibility into objective form, into reality. This would be the sensibility of men and women who do not have to be ashamed of themselves anymore because they have overcome their sense of guilt: they have learned not to identify themselves with the false fathers who have built and tolerated and forgotten the Auschwitzs and Vietnams of history, the torture chambers of all the secular and ecclesiastical inquisitions and interrogations, the ghettos and the monumental temples of the corporations, and who have worshiped the higher culture of this reality. If and when men and women

act and think free from this identification, they will have
broken the chain which linked the fathers and the sons
from generation to generation. They will not have re-
deemed the crimes against humanity, but they will have become free to stop them and to prevent their recommence-
ment. Chance of reaching the point of no return to the past:
if and when the causes are eliminated which have made
the history of mankind the history of domination and servitude. These causes are economic-political, but since they
have shaped the very instincts and needs of men, no economic and political changes will bring this historical continuum to a stop unless they are carried through by men
who are physiologically and psychologically able to experience things, and each other, outside the context of violence and exploitation.

The new sensibility has become, by this very token,
praxis: it emerges in the struggle against violence and exploitation where this struggle is waged for essentially new
ways and forms of life: negation of the entire Establishment, its morality, culture; affirmation of the right to build
a society in which the abolition of poverty and toil terminates in a universe where the sensuous, the playful, the
calm, and the beautiful become forms of existence and
thereby the *Form* of the society itself.

The aesthetic as the possible Form of a free society appears at that stage of development where the intellectual
and material resources for the conquest of scarcity are
available, where previously progressive repression turns
into regressive suppression, where the higher culture in
which the aesthetic values (and the aesthetic truth) had
been monopolized and segregated from the reality col-
lapses and dissolves in desublimated, "lower," and destructive forms, where the hatred of the young bursts into laugh-

ter and song, mixing the barricade and the dance floor, love play and heroism. And the young also attack the *esprit de sérieux* in the socialist camp: miniskirts against the apparat- chiks, rock 'n' roll against Soviet Realism. The insistence that a socialist society can and ought to be light, pretty, playful, that these qualities are essential elements of free- dom, the faith in the rationality of the imagination, the de- mand for a new morality and culture — does this great anti-authoritarian rebellion indicate a new dimension and direction of radical change, the appearance of new agents of radical change, and a new vision of socialism in its qualitative difference from the established societies? Is there anything in the aesthetic dimension which has an essential affinity with freedom not only in its sublimated cultural (artistic) but also in its desublimated political, ex- istential form, so that the aesthetic can become a *gesell- schaftliche Produktivkraft:* factor in the technique of pro- duction, horizon under which the material and intellectual needs develop?

Throughout the centuries, the analysis of the aesthetic dimension focused on the idea of the beautiful. Does this idea express the aesthetic *ethos* which provides the com- mon denominator of the aesthetic and the political?

As desired object, the beautiful pertains to the domain of the primary instincts, Eros and Thanatos. The mythos links the adversaries: pleasure and terror. Beauty has the power to check aggression: it forbids and immobilizes the aggres- sor. The beautiful Medusa petrifies him who confronts her. "Poseidon, the god with azure locks, slept with her in a soft meadow on a bed with springtime flowers." [1] She is slain by Perseus, and from her truncated body springs the

---

[1] Hesiod, *Theogony,* Norman O. Brown, translator (Indianapolis: Bobbs-Merrill, 1953), p. 61.

winged horse Pegasus, symbol of poetic imagination. Kinship of the beautiful, the divine, the poetic, but also kinship of the beautiful and unsublimated joy. Subsequently, the classical aesthetic, while insisting on the harmonious union of sensuousness, imagination, and reason in the beautiful, equally insisted on the objective (ontological) character of the beautiful, as the Form in which man and nature come into their own: fulfillment. Kant asks whether there is not a hidden connection between Beauty and Perfection (*Vollkommenheit*),[2] and Nietzsche notes: "the Beautiful as the mirror (*Spiegelung*) of the Logical, i.e., the laws of logic are the object of the laws of the Beautiful."[3] For the artist, the beautiful is mastery of the opposites "without tension, so that violence is no longer needed. . . ." The beautiful has the "biological value" of that which is "useful, beneficial, enhancing life" (*Lebensteigernd*)."[4]

By virtue of these qualities, the aesthetic dimension can serve as a sort of gauge for a free society. A universe of human relationships no longer mediated by the market, no longer based on competitive exploitation or terror, demands a sensitivity freed from the repressive satisfactions of the unfree societies; a sensitivity receptive to forms and modes of reality which thus far have been projected only by the aesthetic imagination. For the aesthetic needs have their own social content: they are the claims of the human organism, mind and body, for a dimension of fulfillment which can be created only in the struggle against the institutions which, by their very functioning, deny and violate these claims. The radical social content of the aesthetic

[2] Kant, *Handschriftlicher Nachlass* (Akademieausgabe), p. 622.
[3] Nietzsche, *Werke* (Stuttgart: Alfred Kröner, 1921), vol. IX, p. 185.
[4] *Ibid.*, vol. XVI (1911), p. 230.

needs becomes evident as the demand for their most elementary satisfaction is translated into group action on an
enlarged scale. From the harmless drive for better zoning
regulations and a modicum of protection from noise and
dirt to the pressure for closing of whole city areas to automobiles, prohibition of transistor radios in all public places,
decommercialization of nature, total urban reconstruction,
control of the birth rate — such action would become increasingly subversive of the institutions of capitalism and
of their morality. The quantity of such reforms would turn
into the quality of radical change to the degree to which
they would critically weaken the economic, political, and
cultural pressure and power groups which have a vested interest in preserving the environment and ecology of profitable merchandising.

The aesthetic morality is the opposite of puritanism. It
does not insist on a daily bath or shower for people
whose cleaning practices involve systematic torture, slaugh-
tering, poisoning; nor does it insist on clean clothes for men
who are professionally engaged in dirty deals. But it does
insist on cleaning the earth from the very material garbage
produced by the spirit of capitalism, and from this spirit itself. And it insists on freedom as a biological necessity: being physically incapable of tolerating any repression other
than that required for the protection and amelioration of
life.

When Kant, in his third *Critique*, all but obliterated the
frontiers between sensibility and imagination, he recognized the extent to which the senses are "productive," creative — the extent to which they have a share in producing
the images of freedom. For its part, the imagination depends on the senses which provide the experiential material out of which the imagination creates its realm of free-

dom, by transforming the objects and relationships which have been the data of the senses and which have been formed by the senses. The freedom of the imagination is thus restrained by the order of the sensibility, not only by its pure forms (space and time), but also by its empirical content which, as the object-world to be transcended, remains a determining factor in the transcendence. Whatever beautiful or sublime, pleasurable or terrifying forms of reality the imagination may project, they are "derived" from sensuous experience. However, the freedom of the imagination is restrained not only by the sensibility, but also, at the other pole of the organic structure, by the rational faculty of man, his reason. The most daring images of a new world, of new ways of life, are still guided by concepts, and by a logic elaborated in the development of thought, transmitted from generation to generation. On both sides, that of the sensibility and that of reason, history enters into the projects of the imagination, for the world of the senses is a historical world, and reason is the conceptual mastery and interpretation of the historical world.

The order and organization of class society, which have shaped the sensibility and the reason of man, have also shaped the freedom of the imagination. It had its controlled play in the sciences, pure and applied, and its autonomous play in poetry, fiction, the arts. Between the dictates of instrumentalist reason on the one hand and a sense experience mutilated by the realizations of this reason on the other, the power of the imagination was repressed; it was free to become practical, i.e., to transform reality only within the general framework of repression; beyond these limits, the practice of the imagination was violation of taboos of social morality, was perversion and subversion. In the great historical revolutions, the imagination was, for a short period, released and free to enter into the projects of a new social morality and of new institutions of freedom; then it was sacrificed to the requirements of effective reason.

If now, in the rebellion of the young intelligentsia, the right and the truth of the imagination become the demands of political action, if surrealistic forms of protest and refusal spread throughout the movement, this apparently insignificant development may indicate a fundamental change in the situation. The political protest, assuming a total character, reaches into a dimension which, as aesthetic dimension, has been essentially apolitical. And the political protest activates in this dimension precisely the foundational, organic elements: the human sensibility which rebels against the dictates of repressive reason, and, in doing so, invokes the sensuous power of the imagination. The political action which insists on a new morality and a new sensibility as preconditions and results of social change occurs at a point at which the repressive rationality that has brought about the achievements of industrial society becomes utterly regressive — rational only in its efficiency to "contain" liberation. Beyond the limits (and beyond the power) of repressive reason now appears the prospect for a new relationship between sensibility and reason, namely, the harmony between sensibility and a radical consciousness: rational faculties capable of projecting and defining the objective (material) conditions of freedom, its real limits and chances. But instead of being shaped and permeated by the rationality of domination, the sensibility would be guided by the imagination, mediating between the rational faculties and the sensuous needs. The great conception which animates Kant's critical philosophy shatters the philosophical framework in which he kept it. The imagination, unifying sensibility and reason, becomes "productive" as it becomes practical: a guiding force in the reconstruction of reality — reconstruction with the help of a *gaya scienza*, a science and technology released from their service to destruction and exploitation, and thus free for the liberating exigencies of the imagination. The rational transformation of the world could then lead to a reality formed by the aesthetic sensibility of man. Such a world could (in a literal sense!) embody, incorporate, the human faculties and desires to such an extent that they appear as part of the objective determinism of nature — coincidence of causality through nature and causality through freedom. André Breton has made this idea the center of surrealist thought: his concept of the *hasard objectif* designates the nodal point at which the two chains of causation meet and bring about the event.[5]

The aesthetic universe is the *Lebenswelt* on which the needs and faculties of freedom depend for their liberation. They cannot develop in an environment shaped by and for aggressive impulses, nor can they be envisaged as the mere effect of a new set of social institutions. They can emerge only in the collective *practice of creating an environment*: level by level, step by step — in the material and intellectual production, an environment in which the nonaggressive, erotic, receptive faculties of man, in harmony with the consciousness of freedom, strive for the pacification of man and nature. In the reconstruction of society for the attainment of this goal, reality altogether would assume a *Form* ex-

[5] See esp. *Nadja:* "Voici des rencontres qu'explique mal le simple recours à la coïncidence, et qui, comme les rencontres de l'art, productrices de beauté, engendrent un émoi qui parait bien le signe d'une finalité objective, ou, du moins, la marque d'un sens dont nous ne sommes pas les seuls créateurs. Cette finalité, ce sens, supposent, dans le réel, un ordre qui soit leur source. Quel ordre, distinct de l'ordre de la causalité quotidienne, nous est donc ici signifié?" (Ferdinand Alquié, *Philosophie du surréalisme*. Paris: Flammarion, 1955, p. 141).

pressive of the new goal. The essentially aesthetic quality
of this Form would make it a work of *art*, but inasmuch as
the Form is to emerge in the social process of production,
art would have changed its traditional locus and function
in society: it would have become a productive force in the
material as well as cultural transformation. And as such
force, art would be an integral factor in shaping the quality
and the "appearance" of things, in shaping the reality, the
way of life. This would mean the *Aufhebung* of art: end of
the segregation of the aesthetic from the real, but also end
of the commercial unification of business and beauty, exploitation and pleasure. Art would recapture some of its
more primitive "technical" connotations: as the art of pre-
paring (cooking!), cultivating, growing things, giving them
a form which neither violates their matter nor the sensitivity — ascent of Form as one of the necessities of being,
universal beyond all subjective varieties of taste, affinity,
etc. According to Kant, there are pure forms of sensibility
a priori, common to all human beings. Only space and time?
Or is there perhaps also a more material constitutive form,
such as the primary distinction between beautiful and ugly,
good and bad [6] — prior to all rationalization and ideology,
a distinction made by the senses (productive in their receptivity), distinguishing that which violates sensibility
from that which gratifies it? In which case the vast varieties
of taste, affinity, predilection would be the differentiation of
an "original" basic form of sensibility, sense experience, on
which modeling, restraining, and repressing forces would
operate in accord with the respective individual and social
situation.

The new sensibility and the new consciousness which are

[6] Here too, Kant's aesthetic theory leads to the most advanced notions:
the beautiful as "symbol" of the moral.

to project and guide such reconstruction demand a new
language to define and communicate the new "values" (language in the wider sense which includes words, images,
gestures, tones). It has been said that the degree to which
a revolution is developing *qualitatively* different social
conditions and relationships may perhaps be indicated by
the development of a different language: the rupture with
the continuum of domination must also be a rupture with
the vocabulary of domination. The surrealist thesis, according to which the poet is the total nonconformist, finds in the
poetic language the semantic elements of the revolution.

> Car le poète . . . ne peut plus être reconnu comme tel s'il
> ne s'oppose par un non-conformisme total au monde où il
> vit. Il se dresse contre tous, y compris les révolutionnaires
> qui, se plaçant sur le terrain de la seule politique, arbitrairement isolée par là de l'ensemble du mouvement culturel — préconisent la soumission de la culture à l'accomplissement de la révolution sociale.[7]

The surrealist thesis does not abandon the materialistic
premises but it protests against the isolation of the material
from the cultural development, which leads to a submission
of the latter to the former and thus to a reduction (if not
denial) of the libertarian possibilities of the revolution.
Prior to their incorporation into the material development,
these possibilities are "sur-realistic": they belong to the
poetic imagination, formed and expressed in the poetic language. It is not, it cannot be, an instrumentalist language,
not an instrument of revolution.

It seems that the poems and the songs of protest and liberation are always too late or too early: memory or dream.

[7] Benjamin Péret, *Le Déshonneur des poètes* (Paris: Pauvert, 1965),
p. 65. Written in 1943.

Their time is not the present; they preserve their truth in their hope, in their refusal of the actual. The distance between the universe of poetry and that of politics is so great, the mediations which validate the poetic truth and the rationality of imagination are so complex, that any shortcut between the two realities seems fatal to poetry. There is no way in which we can envisage a historical change in the relation between the cultural and the revolutionary movement which could bridge the gap between the everyday and the poetic language and abrogate the dominance of the former. The latter seems to draw all its power and all its truth from its otherness, its transcendence.

And yet, the radical denial of the Establishment and the communication of the new consciousness depend more and more fatefully on a language of their own as all communication is monopolized and validated by the one-dimensional society. To be sure, the language of denial has, in its "material," always been the same as the language of affirmation; the linguistic continuity reasserted itself after every revolution. Perhaps necessarily so, because through all revolutions, the continuity of domination has been sustained. But in the past, the language of indictment and liberation, though it shared its vocabulary with the masters and their retainers, had found its own meaning and validation in actual revolutionary struggles which eventually changed the established societies. The familiar (used and abused) vocabulary of freedom, justice, and equality could thus obtain not only new meaning but also new reality — the reality which emerged in the revolutions of the 17th and 18th centuries and led to less restricted forms of freedom, justice, and equality.

Today, the rupture with the linguistic universe of the Establishment is more radical: in the most militant areas of protest, it amounts to a methodical reversal of meaning. It is a familiar phenomenon that subcultural groups develop their own language, taking the harmless words of everyday communication out of their context and using them for designating objects or activities tabooed by the Establishment. This is the Hippie subculture: "trip," "grass," "pot," "acid," and so on. But a far more subversive universe of discourse announces itself in the language of black militants. Here is a systematic linguistic rebellion, which smashes the ideological context in which the words are employed and defined, and places them into the opposite context — negation of the established one.[8] Thus, the blacks "take over" some of the most sublime and sublimated concepts of Western civilization, desublimate them, and redefine them. For ex-

[8] The familiar "obscenities" in the language of the black and white radicals must be seen in this context of a methodical subversion of the linguistic universe of the Establishment. "Obscenities" are not officially co-opted and sanctioned by the spoken and written professions of the powers that be; their usage thus breaks the false ideological language and invalidates its definitions. But only in the political context of the Great Refusal do obscenities perform this function. If, for example, the highest executives of the nation or of the state are called, not President X or Governor Y but pig X or pig Y, and if what they say in campaign speeches is rendered as "oink, oink," this offensive designation is used to deprive them of the aura of public servants or leaders who have only the common interest in mind. They are "redefined" as that which they really are in the eyes of the radicals. And if they are addressed as men who have perpetrated the unspeakable Oedipal crime, they are indicted on the counts of their own morality: the order they enforce with such violence was born in their sense of guilt. They slept with the mother without having slain the father, a deed less reprehensible but more contemptible than that of Oedipus. The methodical use of "obscenities" in the political language of the radicals is the elemental act of giving a new name to men and things, obliterating the false and hypocritical name which the renamed figures proudly bear in and for the system. And if the renaming invokes the sexual sphere, it falls in line with the great design of the desublimation of culture, which, to the radicals, is a vital aspect of liberation.

ample, the "soul" (in its essence lily-white ever since
Plato), the traditional seat of everything that is truly human
in man, tender, deep, immortal — the word which has become embarrassing, corny, false in the established universe of discourse, has been desublimated and in this trans-
substantiation, migrated to the Negro culture: they are
soul brothers; the soul is black, violent, orgiastic; it is no
longer in Beethoven, Schubert, but in the blues, in jazz, in
rock 'n' roll, in "soul food." Similarly, the militant slogan
"black is beautiful" redefines another central concept of the
traditional culture by reversing its symbolic value and as-
sociating it with the anti-color of darkness, tabooed magic,
the uncanny. The ingression of the aesthetic into the political also appears at the other pole of the rebellion against
the society of affluent capitalism, among the nonconformist
youth. Here, too, the reversal of meaning, driven to the
point of open contradiction: giving flowers to the police,
"flower power" — the redefinition and very negation of the
sense of "power"; the erotic belligerency in the songs of
protest; the sensuousness of long hair, of the body unsoiled
by plastic cleanliness.

These political manifestations of a new sensibility indicate the depth of the rebellion, of the rupture with the continuum of repression. They bear witness to the power of
the society in shaping the whole of experience, the whole
metabolism between the organism and its environment.
Beyond the physiological level, the exigencies of sensibility
develop as historical ones: the objects which the senses confront and apprehend are the products of a specific stage of
civilization and of a specific society, and the senses in turn
are geared to their objects. This historical interrelation
affects even the primary sensations: an established society
imposes upon all its members the same medium of percep-

tion; and through all the differences of individual and class perspectives, horizons, backgrounds, society provides the same general universe of experience. Consequently, the rupture with the continuum of aggression and exploitation would also break with the sensibility geared to this universe. Today's rebels want to see, hear, feel new things in a new way: they link liberation with the dissolution of ordinary and orderly perception. The "trip" involves the dissolution of the ego shaped by the established society — an artificial and short-lived dissolution. But the artificial and "private" liberation anticipates, in a distorted manner, an exigency of the social liberation: the revolution must be at the same time a revolution in perception which will accompany the material and intellectual reconstruction of society, creating the new aesthetic environment.

Awareness of the need for such a revolution in perception, for a new sensorium, is perhaps the kernel of truth in the psychedelic search. But it is vitiated when its narcotic character brings temporary release not only from the reason and rationality of the established system but also from that other rationality which is to change the established system, when sensibility is freed not only from the exigencies of the existing order but also from those of liberation. Intentionally noncommitted, the withdrawal creates its artificial paradises within the society from which it withdrew. They thus remain subject to the law of this society, which punishes the inefficient performances. In contrast, the radical transformation of society implies the union of the new sensibility with a new rationality. The imagination becomes productive if it becomes the mediator between sensibility on the one hand, and theoretical as well as practical reason on the other, and in this harmony of faculties (in which Kant saw the token of freedom) guides the reconstruction of society. Such a union has been the distinguishing feature of *art,* but its realization has been stopped at the point at which it would have become incompatible with the basic institutions and social relationships. The material culture, the reality, continued to lag behind the progress of reason and imagination and to condemn much of these faculties to irreality, fantasy, fiction. Art could not become a technique in reconstructing reality; the sensibility remained repressed, and the experience mutilated. But the revolt against repressive reason which released the chained power of the aesthetic in the new sensibility has also radicalized it in art: the value and function of art are undergoing essential changes. They affect the affirmative character of art (by virtue of which art has the power of reconciliation with the *status quo*), and the degree of sublimation (which militated against the realization of the truth, of the cognitive force of art). The protest against these features of art spreads through the entire universe of art prior to the First World War and continues with increased intensity: it gives voice and image to the negative power of art, and to the tendencies toward a desublimation of culture.

The emergence of contemporary art (I shall use "art" throughout as including the visual arts as well as literature and music) means more than the traditional replacement of one style by another. Non-objective, abstract painting and sculpture, stream-of-consciousness and formalist literature, twelve-tone composition, blues and jazz: these are not merely new modes of perception reorienting and intensifying the old ones; they rather dissolve the very structure of perception in order to make room — for what? The new object of art is not yet "given," but the familiar object has become impossible, false. From illusion, imitation, harmony to reality — but the reality is not yet "given"; it is not the one which is the object of "realism." Reality has to be discovered and projected. The senses must learn not to see things anymore in the medium of that law and order which has formed them; the bad functionalism which organizes our sensibility must be smashed.

From the beginning, the new art insists on its radical autonomy in tension or conflict with the development of the Bolshevik Revolution and the revolutionary movements activated by it. Art remains alien to the revolutionary praxis by virtue of the artist's commitment to Form: Form as art's own reality, as *die Sache selbst*. The Russian "formalist" B. Eikhenbaum insists:

> La notion de forme a obtenu un sens nouveau, elle n'est plus une enveloppe, mais une intégrité dynamique et concrète qui a un contenu en elle-même, hors de toute corrélation.[9]

Form is the achievement of the artistic perception which breaks the unconscious and "false" "automatism," the unquestioned familiarity which operates in every practice, including the revolutionary practice — an automatism of immediate experience, but a socially engineered experience which militates against the liberation of sensibility. The artistic perception is supposed to shatter this immediacy which, in truth, is a historical product: the medium of experience imposed by the established society but coagulating into a self-sufficient, closed, "automatic" system:

> Ainsi la vie disparaît, se transformant en un rien. L'automatisation avale les objets, les habits, les meubles, la femme et la peur de la guerre.[10]

[9] B. Eikhenbaum, in *Theorie de la Littérature*. Textes des Formalistes Russes, ed. Tzvetan Todorov (Paris: Editions du Seuil, 1965), p. 44.
[10] V. Chklovski, in *ibid.*, p. 83.

If this deadly system of life is to be changed without being replaced by another deadly one, men must learn to develop the new sensibility of life — of their own life and that of things:

> Et voilà que pour rendre la sensation de la vie, pour sentir les objets, pour éprouver que la pierre est de pierre, il existe ce que l'on appelle l'art. Le but de l'art, c'est de donner une sensation de l'objet comme vision et non pas comme reconnaissance; le procédé de l'art est le procédé de singularisation des objets et le procédé qui consiste à obscurcir la forme, à augmenter la difficulté et la durée de la perception. L'acte de perception en art est une fin en soi et doit être prolongé; *l'art est un moyen d'éprouver le devenir de l'objet; ce qui est déjà 'devenu', n'importe pas pour l'art.*[11]

I have referred to the Formalists because it seems characteristic that the transformative element in art is emphasized by a school which insists on the artistic perception as end-in-itself, on the Form as Content. It is precisely the Form by virtue of which art transcends the given reality, works in the established reality against the established reality; and this transcendent element is inherent in art, in the artistic dimension. Art alters experience by reconstructing the objects of experience — reconstructing them in word, tone, image. Why? Evidently, the "language" of art must communicate a truth, an objectivity which is not accessible to ordinary language and ordinary experience. This exigency explodes in the situation of contemporary art.

The radical character, the "violence" of this reconstruction in contemporary art seems to indicate that it does not rebel against one style or another but against "style" itself,

[11] *Ibid.*

against the art-form of art, against the traditional "meaning" of art.

The great artistic rebellion in the period of the first World
War gives the signal.

> Wir setzen grossen Jahrhunderten ein Nein entgegen . . .
> (Wir) gehen, zur spöttischen Verwunderung unserer Mit-
> welt, einen Seitenweg, der kaum ein Weg zu sein scheint,
> und sagen: Dies ist die Hauptstrasse der Menschheitsent-
> wicklung.[12]

The fight is against the "Illusionistische Kunst Europas": [13]
art must no longer be illusory because its relation to reality
has changed: the latter has become susceptible to, even
dependent on, the transforming function of art. The revolutions and the defeated and betrayed revolutions which occurred in the wake of the war denounced a reality which
had made art an illusion, and inasmuch as art has been an
illusion (*schöner Schein*), the new art proclaims itself as
anti-art. Moreover, the illusory art incorporated the established ideas of possession (*Besitzvorstellungen*) naïvely
into its forms of representation: it did not question the
object-character (*die Dinglichkeiten*) of the world as subject to man. Art must break with this reification: it must
become *gemalte oder modellierte Erkenntniskritik*, based
on a new optic replacing the Newtonian optic, and this art
would correspond to a "type of man who is not like us." [14]
Since then, the eruption of anti-art in art has manifested
itself in many familar forms: destruction of syntax, frag-
mentation of words and sentences, explosive use of ordinary

---

[12] Franz Marc, "Der Blaue Reiter" (1914), in *Manifeste Manifeste
1905–1933* (Dresden: Verlag der Kunst, 1956), p. 56.
[13] Raoul Hausmann, "Die Kunst und die Zeit," 1919 (in *ibid.*, p. 186).
[14] *Ibid.*, pp. 188 ff.

language, compositions without score, sonatas for anything. And yet, this entire de-formation is Form: anti-art has remained art, supplied, purchased, and contemplated as art.

The wild revolt of art has remained a short-lived shock, quickly absorbed in the art gallery, within the four walls, in the concert hall, by the market, and adorning the plazas and lobbies of the prospering business establishments. Transforming the intent of art is self-defeating — a self-defeat built into the very structure of art. No matter how affirmative, "realistic" the oeuvre may be, the artist has given it a form which is not part of the reality he presents and in which he works. The oeuvre is unreal precisely inasmuch as it is art: the novel is not a newspaper story, the still life not alive, and even in pop art the real tin can is not in the supermarket. The very Form of art contradicts the effort to do away with the segregation of art to a "second reality," to translate the truth of the productive imagination into the first reality.

The Form of art: we must once again glance at the philosophical tradition which has focused the analysis of art on the concept of the "beautiful" (in spite of the fact that so much of art is obviously not beautiful!). The beautiful has been interpreted as ethical and cognitive "value": the *kalokagathon;* the beautiful as sensuous appearance of the Idea; the Way of Truth passes through the realm of the Beautiful. What is meant by these metaphors?

The root of the aesthetic is in sensibility. What is beautiful is first sensuous: it appeals to the senses; it is pleasurable, object of unsublimated drives. However, the beautiful seems to occupy a position halfway between sublimated and unsublimated objectives. Beauty is not an essential, "organic" feature of the immediate sex-object (it may even deter the unsublimated drive!), while, at the other extreme, a mathematical theorem can be called "beautiful" only in a highly abstract, figurative sense. It seems that the various connotations of beauty converge in the idea of *Form*.

In the aesthetic Form, the content (matter) is assembled, defined, and arranged to obtain a condition in which the immediate, unmastered forces of the matter, of the "material," are mastered, "ordered." Form is the negation, the mastery of disorder, violence, suffering, even when it presents disorder, violence, suffering. This triumph of art is achieved by subjecting the content to the aesthetic order, which is autonomous in its exigencies. The work of art sets its own limits and ends, it is *sinngebend* in relating the elements to each other according to its own law: the "form" of the tragedy, novel, sonata, picture . . . The content is thereby transformed: it obtains a meaning (sense) which transcends the elements of the content, and this transcending order is the appearance of the beautiful as the truth of art. The way in which the tragedy narrates the fate of Oedipus and the city, in which it orders the sequence of events, gives word to the unsaid and to the unspeakable — the "Form" of the tragedy terminates the horror with the end of the play — it brings the destruction to a standstill, it makes the blind seeing, the intolerable tolerable and understandable, it subordinates the wrong, the contingent, the evil, to "poetic justice." The phrase is indicative of the internal ambivalence of art: to indict that which is, and to "cancel" the indictment in the aesthetic form, redeeming the suffering, the crime. This "redeeming," reconciling power seems inherent in art, by virtue of its being art, by virtue of its form-giving power.

The redeeming, reconciling power of art adheres even to the most radical manifestations of non-illusory art and anti-art. They are still oeuvres: paintings, sculptures, compositions, poems, and as such they have their own form and with it their own order: their own frame (though it may be invisible), their own space, their own beginning, and their own end. The aesthetic necessity of art supersedes the terrible necessity of reality, sublimates its pain and pleasure; the blind suffering and cruelty of nature (and of the "nature" of man) assume meaning and end — "poetic justice." The horror of the crucifixion is purified by the beautiful face of Jesus dominating the beautiful composition, the horror of politics by the beautiful verse of Racine, the horror of farewell forever by the *Lied von der Erde*. And in this aesthetic universe, joy and fulfillment find their proper place alongside pain and death — everything is in order again. The indictment is canceled, and even defiance, insult, and derision — the extreme artistic negation of art — succumb to this order.

With this restoration of order, the Form indeed achieves a *katharsis* — the terror and the pleasure of reality are purified. But the achievement is illusory, false, fictitious: it remains within the dimension of art, a work of art; in reality, fear and frustration go on unabated (as they do, after the brief *katharsis*, in the psyche). This is perhaps the most telling expression of the contradiction, the self-defeat, built into art: the pacifying conquest of matter, the transfiguration of the object remain unreal — just as the revolution in perception remains unreal. And this vicarious character of art has, time and again, given rise to the question as to the justification of art: was the Parthenon worth the sufferings of a single slave? Is it possible to write poetry after Auschwitz? The question has been countered: when the horror of reality tends to become total and blocks political action, where else than in the radical imagination, as refusal of reality, can the rebellion, and its uncompromised goals, be remembered? But today, are the images and their realization still the domain of "illusory" art?

We suggested the historical possibility of conditions in which the aesthetic could become a *gesellschaftliche Produktivkraft* and as such could lead to the "end" of art through its realization. Today, the outline of such conditions appears only in the negativity of the advanced industrial societies. They are societies whose capabilities defy the imagination. No matter what sensibility art may wish to develop, no matter what Form it may wish to give to things, to life, no matter what vision it may wish to communicate — a radical change of experience is within the technical reaches of powers whose terrible imagination organizes the world in their own image and perpetuates, ever bigger and better, the mutilated experience.

However, the productive forces, chained in the infrastructure of these societies, counteract this negativity in progress. To be sure, the libertarian possibilities of technology and science are effectively contained within the framework of the given reality: the calculated projection and engineering of human behavior, the frivolous invention of waste and luxurious junk, the experimentation with the limits of endurance and destruction are tokens of the mastery of necessity in the interest of exploitation — which indicate nevertheless progress in the mastery of necessity. Released from the bondage to exploitation, the imagination, sustained by the achievements of science, could turn its productive power to the radical reconstruction of experience and the universe of experience. In this reconstruction, the historical *topos* of the aesthetic would change: it would find expression in the transformation of the *Lebenswelt* — society as a work of art. This "utopian" goal depends (as every stage in the development of freedom did) on a revolution at the attainable level of liberation. In other words: the transformation is conceivable only as the way in which free men (or rather men in the practice of freeing themselves) shape their life in solidarity, and build an environment in which the struggle for existence loses its ugly and aggressive features. The Form of freedom is not merely self-determination and self-realization, but rather the determination and realization of goals which enhance, protect, and unite life on earth. And this autonomy would find expression not only in the mode of production and production relations but also in the individual relations among men, in their language and in their silence, in their gestures and their looks, in their sensitivity, in their love and hate. The beautiful would be an essential quality of their freedom.

But today's rebels against the established culture also rebel against the beautiful in this culture, against its all too sublimated, segregated, orderly, harmonizing forms. Their libertarian aspirations appear as the negation of the traditional culture: as a methodical desublimation. Perhaps its strongest impetus comes from social groups which thus far have remained outside the entire realm of the higher culture, outside its affirmative, sublimating, and justifying magic — human beings who have lived in the shadow of this culture, the victims of the power structure which has been the basis of this culture. They now oppose to the "music of the spheres" which was the most sublime achievement of this culture their own music, with all the defiance, and the hatred, and the joy of rebellious victims, defining their own humanity against the definitions of the masters. The black music, invading the white culture, is the terrifying realization of *"O Freunde, nicht diese Töne!"* — the refusal now hits the chorus which sings the Ode to Joy, the song which is invalidated in the culture that sings it. Thomas Mann's *Doctor Faustus* knows it: "I want to revoke the Ninth Symphony." In the subversive, dissonant, crying and shouting rhythm, born in the "dark continent" and in the "deep South" of slavery and deprivation, the oppressed revoke the Ninth Symphony and give art a desublimated, sensuous form of frightening immediacy, moving, electrifying the body, and the soul materialized in the body. Black music is originally music of the oppressed, illuminating the extent to which the higher culture and its sublime sublimations, its beauty, have been class-based. The affinity between black music (and its avant-gardistic white development) and the political rebellion against the "affluent society" bears witness to the increasing desublimation of culture.

It is still the simple, elementary negation, the antithesis: position of the immediate denial. This desublimation leaves the traditional culture, the illusionist art behind unmastered: their truth and their claims remain valid — next to and together with the rebellion, within the same given society. The rebellious music, literature, art are thus easily absorbed and shaped by the market — rendered harmless. In order to come into their own, they would have to abandon the direct appeal, the raw immediacy of their presentation, which invokes, in the protest, the familiar universe of politics and business, and with it the helpless familiarity of frustration and temporary release from frustration. Was it not precisely the rupture with this familarity which was the methodical goal of radical art? The abrogation of the Estrangement Effect (which, to a considerable extent, was also operative in the great illusionist art) defeats the radicalism of today's art. Thus, the "living theater" founders to the degree to which it is living, to which we immediately identify ourselves with the actors, experience our familiar sympathies, empathies, antipathies. The theater does not transcend this familiarity, this "déjà vu" — it strengthens it. Just like the more and more organized "happenings," like the ever more marketable pop art, this *ambiance* creates a deceptive "community" within the society.

The conquest of this immediate familiarity, the "mediations" which would make the many forms of rebellious art a liberating force on the societal scale (that is to say, a subverting force) are yet to be attained. They would reside in modes of work and pleasure, of thought and behavior, in a technology and in a natural environment which express the aesthetic ethos of socialism. Then, art may have lost its privileged, and segregated, dominion over the imagination, the beautiful, the dream. This may be the future, but the future ingresses into the present: in its negativity, the desublimating art and anti-art of today "anticipate" a stage where society's capacity to produce may be akin to the creative capacity of art, and the construction of the world of art akin to the reconstruction of the real world — union of liberating art and liberating technology.[15] By virtue of this anticipation, the disorderly, uncivil, farcical, artistic desublimation of culture constitutes an essential element of radical politics: of the subverting forces in transition.

[15] A utopian vision indeed, but realistic enough to animate the militant students of the Ecole des Beaux Arts in their action of May 1968: they called for a development of a consciousness which would guide the "creative activity immanent in every individual," so that the "work of art" and "the artist" become mere "moments in this activity" — moments which are paralyzed in every social "system which makes the work or the man into a monument" (*Quelle université? Quelle société?*, *loc. cit.*, p. 123).

III. Subverting Forces
— in Transition

The notion of "aesthetic form" as the Form of a free society would indeed mean reversing the development of socialism from scientific to utopian unless we can point to certain tendencies in the infrastructure of advanced industrial society which may give this notion a realistic content. We have repeatedly referred to such tendencies: first of all the growing technological character of the process of production, with the reduction of the required physical energy and its replacement by mental energy — dematerialization of labor. At the same time, an increasingly automated machine system, no longer used as the system of exploitation, would allow that "distantiation" of the laborer from the instruments of production which Marx foresaw at the end of capitalism: the workers would cease to be the "principal agents" of material production, and become its "supervisors and regulators" — the emergence of a free subject within the realm of necessity. Already today, the achievements of science and technology permit the play of the productive imagination: experimentation with the possibilities of form and matter hitherto enclosed in the density of unmastered nature; the technical transformation of nature tends to make things lighter, easier, prettier — the loosening up of reification. The material becomes increasingly susceptible and subject to aesthetic forms, which enhance its exchange value (the artistic, modernistic banks, office buildings, kitchens, salesrooms, and salespeople, etc.). And within the framework of capitalism, the tremendous growth in the productivity of labor enforces the ever-enlarged production of "luxuries": wasteful in the armament industry, and in the marketing of gadgets, devices, trimmings, status symbols.

This same trend of production and consumption, which makes for the affluence and attraction of advanced capitalism, makes for the perpetuation of the struggle for existence, for the increasing necessity to produce and consume the non-necessary: the growth of the so-called "discretionary income" in the United States indicates the extent to which income earned is spent on other than "basic needs." Former luxuries become basic needs, a normal development which, under corporate capitalism, extends the competitive business of living to newly created needs and satisfactions. The fantastic output of all sorts of things and services defies the imagination, while restricting and distorting it in the commodity form, through which capitalist production enlarges its hold over human existence. And yet, precisely through the spread of this commodity form, the repressive social morality which sustains the system is being weakened. The obvious contradiction between the liberating possibilities of the technological transformation of the world, the light and free life on the one hand and the intensification of the struggle for existence on the other, generates among the underlying population that diffused aggressiveness which, unless steered to hate and fight the alleged national enemy, hits upon any suitable target: white or black, native or foreigner, Jew or Christian, rich or poor.

This is the aggressiveness of those with the mutilated experience, with the false consciousness and the false needs, the victims of repression who, for their living, depend on the repressive society and repress the alternative. Their violence is that of the Establishment and takes as targets figures which, rightly or wrongly, seem to be different, and to represent an alternative.

But while the image of the libertarian potential of advanced industrial society is repressed (and hated) by the managers of repression and their consumers, it motivates the radical opposition and gives it its strange unorthodox character. Very different from the revolution at previous stages of history, this opposition is directed against the totality of a well-functioning, prosperous society — a protest against its Form — the commodity form of men and things, against the imposition of false values and a false morality. This new consciousness and the instinctual rebellion isolate such opposition from the masses and from the majority of organized labor, the integrated majority, and make for the concentration of radical politics in active minorities, mainly among the young middle-class intelligentsia, and among the ghetto populations. Here, prior to all political strategy and organization, liberation becomes a vital, "biological" need.

It is of course nonsense to say that middle-class opposition is replacing the proletariat as the revolutionary class, and that the *Lumpenproletariat* is becoming a radical political force. What is happening is the formation of still relatively small and weakly organized (often disorganized) groups which, by virtue of their consciousness and their needs, function as potential catalysts of rebellion within the majorities to which, by their class origin, they belong. In this sense, the militant intelligentsia has indeed cut

itself loose from the middle classes, and the ghetto population from the organized working class. But by that token
they do not think and act in a vacuum: their consciousness
and their goals make them representatives of the very real
common interest of the oppressed. As against the rule of
class and national interests which suppress this common interest, the revolt against the old societies is truly international: emergence of a new, spontaneous solidarity. This
struggle is a far cry from the ideal of humanism and hu-
manitas; it is the struggle for life — life not as masters and
not as slaves, but as men and women.

For Marxian theory, the location (or rather contraction)
of the opposition in certain middle-class strata and in the
ghetto population appears as an intolerable deviation — as
does the emphasis on biological and aesthetic needs: regression to bourgeois or, even worse, aristocratic, ideolo-
gies. But, in the advanced monopoly-capitalist countries,
the displacement of the opposition (from the organized industrial working classes to militant minorities) is caused by
the internal development of the society; and the theoretical
"deviation" only reflects this development. What appears
as a surface phenomenon is indicative of basic tendencies
which suggest not only different prospects of change, but
also a depth and extent of change far beyond the expecta-
tions of traditional socialist theory. Under this aspect, the
displacement of the negating forces from their traditional
base among the underlying population, rather than being
a sign of the weakness of the opposition against the integrating power of advanced capitalism, may well be the slow
formation of a new base, bringing to the fore the new historical Subject of change, responding to the new objective
conditions, with qualitatively different needs and aspirations. And on this base (probably intermittent and prelim-

inary) goals and strategies take shape which reexamine the concepts of democratic-parliamentary as well as of revolutionary transformation.

The modifications in the structure of capitalism alter the basis for the development and organization of potentially revolutionary forces. Where the traditional laboring classes cease to be the "gravediggers" of capitalism, this function remains, as it were, suspended, and the political efforts toward change remain "tentative," preparatory not only in a temporal but also in a structural sense. This means that the "addressees" as well as the immediate goals and occasions of action will be determined by the shifting situation rather than by a theoretically well-founded and elaborated strategy. This determinism, direct consequence of the strength of the system and the diffusion of the opposition, also implies a shift of emphasis toward "subjective factors": the development of awareness and needs assumes primary importance. Under total capitalist administration and introjection, the social determination of consciousness is all but complete and immediate: direct implantation of the latter into the former. Under these circumstances, radical change in consciousness is the beginning, the first step in changing social existence: emergence of the new Subject. Historically, it is again the period of enlightenment prior to material change — a period of education, but education which turns into praxis: demonstration, confrontation, rebellion.

The radical transformation of a social system still depends on the class which constitutes the human base of the process of production. In the advanced capitalist countries, this is the industrial working class. The changes in the composition of this class, and the extent of its integration into the system alter, not the potential but the actual political role of labor. Revolutionary class "in-itself" but not "for-itself," objectively but not subjectively, its radicalization will depend on catalysts outside its ranks. The development of a radical political consciousness among the masses is conceivable only if and when the economic stability and the social cohesion of the system begin to weaken. It was the traditional role of the Marxist-Leninist party to prepare the ground for this development. The stabilizing and integrating power of advanced capitalism, and the requirements of "peaceful coexistence," forced this party to "parliamentarize" itself, to integrate itself into the bourgeois-democratic process, and to concentrate on economic demands, thereby inhibiting rather than promoting the growth of a radical political consciousness. Where the latter broke through the party and trade union apparatus, it happened under the impact of "outside" forces — mainly from among the intelligentsia; the apparatus only followed suit when the movement gained momentum, and in order to regain control of it.

No matter how rational this strategy may be, no matter how sensible the desperate effort to preserve strength in the face of the sustained power of corporate capitalism, the strategy testifies to the "passivity" of the industrial working classes, to the degree of their integration — it testifies to the facts which the official theory so vehemently denies. Under the conditions of integration, the new political consciousness of the vital need for radical change emerges among social groups which, on objective grounds, are (relatively) free from the integrating, conservative interests and aspirations, free for the radical transvaluation of values. Without losing its historical role as the basic force of transformation, the working class, in the period of stabilization, assumes a stabilizing, conservative function; and the catalysts of transformation operate "from without."

This tendency is strengthened by the changing composition of the working class. The declining proportion of blue collar labor, the increasing number and importance of white collar employees, technicians, engineers, and specialists, divides the class. This means that precisely those strata of the working class which bore, and still bear, the brunt of brute exploitation will perform a gradually diminishing function in the process of production. The intelligentsia obtains an increasingly decisive role in this process — an instrumentalist intelligentsia, but intelligentsia nevertheless. This "new working class," by virtue of its position, could disrupt, reorganize, and redirect the mode and relationships of production. However, they have neither the interest nor the vital need to do so: they are well integrated and well rewarded.[1] To be sure, monopolistic competition and the race for intensifying the productivity of labor may enforce technological changes which may come into conflict with still prevailing policies and forms of private capitalist enterprise, and these changes may then lead to a technocratic reorganization of large sectors of the society

[1] On June 15, 1967, *The New York Times* published, under the heading "Think Tanks: Applied Research on Not for Profit Basis Is Paying Off Handsomely," an article on the $29 million a year Illinois Institute of Technology Research Institute [sic]. One "of the hundreds of engineers" interviewed by the writer is quoted as follows: "There is a tremendous amount of selling in this job. . . . My real love is minimum weight structures . . . but I'm willing to work on minimum cost structures or how to kill the Russians better because the organization survives by doing research that's saleable." This statement, priceless in itself and a treasure for language analysis (note the smooth fusion of love, kill, research, and saleable), expresses the consciousness (and the unconscious) of at least one of these "technocrats." Potential revolutionaries?

(even of its culture and ideology). But it is not clear why they would lead to an abolition of the capitalist system, of the subjugation of the underlying population to the apparatus of profitable production for particular interests. Such a qualitative change would presuppose the control and redirection of the productive apparatus by groups with needs and goals very different from those of the technocrats.[2] Technocracy, no matter how "pure," sustains and streamlines the continuum of domination. This fatal link can be cut only by a revolution which makes technology and technique subservient to the needs and goals of free men: in this sense, and in this sense only, it would be a revolution against technocracy.

Such a revolution is not on the agenda. In the domain of corporate capitalism, the two historical factors of transformation, the subjective and objective, do not coincide: they are prevalent in different and even antagonistic groups. The objective factor, i.e., the human base of the process of production which reproduces the established society, exists in the industrial working class, the human source and reservoir of exploitation; the subjective factor, i.e., the political consciousness exists among the nonconformist young intelligentsia; and the vital need for change is the very life of the ghetto population; and of the "underprivileged" sections of the laboring classes in backward capitalist countries. The two historical factors do coincide in large areas of the Third World, where the National Liberation Fronts and the guerrillas fight with the support and participation of the class which is the base of the process of production, namely, the predominantly agrarian and the emerging industrial proletariat.

---

[2] The existence of such groups among the highly qualified technical personnel was demonstrated during the May–June rebellion in France.

The constellation which prevails in the metropoles of capitalism, namely, the objective necessity of radical change, and the paralysis of the masses, seems typical of a nonrevolutionary but prerevolutionary situation. The transition from the former to the latter presupposes a critical weakening of the global economy of capitalism, and the intensification and extension of the political work: radical enlightenment. It is precisely the preparatory character of this work which gives it its historical significance: to develop, in the exploited, the consciousness (and the unconscious) which would loosen the hold of enslaving needs over their existence — the needs which perpetuate their dependence on the system of exploitation. Without this rupture, which can only be the result of political education in action, even the most elemental, the most immediate force of rebellion may be defeated, or become the mass basis of counterrevolution.

The ghetto population of the United States constitutes such a force. Confined to small areas of living and dying, it can be more easily organized and directed. Moreover, located in the core cities of the country, the ghettos form natural geographical centers from which the struggle can be mounted against targets of vital economic and political importance; in this respect, the ghettos can be compared with the *faubourgs* of Paris in the eighteenth century, and their location makes for spreading and "contagious" upheavals. Cruel and indifferent privation is now met with increasing resistance, but its still largely unpolitical character facilitates suppression and diversion. The racial conflict still separates the ghettos from the allies outside. While it is true that the white man is guilty, it is equally true that white men are rebels and radicals. However, the fact is that monopolistic imperialism validates the racist thesis: it sub-

jects ever more nonwhite populations to the brutal power of
its bombs, poisons, and moneys; thus making even the exploited white population in the metropoles partners and
beneficiaries of the global crime. Class conflicts are being
superseded or blotted out by race conflicts: color lines become economic and political realities — a development
rooted in the dynamic of late imperialism and its struggle
for new methods of internal and external colonization.

The long-range power of the black rebellion is further
threatened by the deep division within this class (the rise of
a Negro bourgeoisie), and by its marginal (in terms of the
capitalist system) social function. The majority of the black
population does not occupy a decisive position in the process of production, and the white organizations of labor have
not exactly gone out of their way to change this situation.
In the cynical terms of the system, a large part of this population is "expendable," that is to say, it makes no essential
contribution to the productivity of the system. Consequently, the powers that be may not hesitate to apply extreme measures of suppression if the movement becomes
dangerous. The fact is that, at present in the United States,
the black population appears as the "most natural" force of
rebellion.

Its distance from the young middle-class opposition is
formidable in every respect. The common ground: the total
rejection of the existing society, of its entire value system,
is obscured by the obvious class difference — just as, within
the white population, the community of "real interest" between the students and the workers is vitiated by the class
conflict. However, this community did realize itself in political action on a rather large scale during the May rebellion in France — against the implicit injunction on the part
of the Communist Party and the CGT (*Confédération*

Générale du Travail), and the common action was ini-
tiated by the students, not by the workers. This fact may be
indicative of the depth and unity of the opposition under-
neath and across the class conflicts. With respect to the student movement, a basic trend in the very stucture of advanced industrial society favors the gradual development
of such a community of interests. The long-range process
which, in large areas of material production, tends to replace heavy physical labor by technical, mental energy, in-
creases the social need for scientifically trained, intelligent
workers; a considerable part of the student population is
prospective working class — "new working class," not only
not expendable, but vital for the growth of the existing society. The student rebellion hits this society at a vulnerable
point; accordingly, the reaction is venomous and violent.

The "student movement" — the very term is already ideological and derogatory: it conceals the fact that quite important sections of the older intelligentsia and of the non-
student population take active part in the movement. It
proclaims very different goals and aspirations; the general
demands for educational reforms are only the immediate
expression of wider and more fundamental aims. The most
decisive difference is between the opposition in the socialist and that in the capitalist countries. The former
accepts the socialist structure of society but protests against
the repressive-authoritarian regime of the state and party
bureaucracy; while, in the capitalist countries, the militant
(and apparently increasing) part of the movement is anti-
capitalist: socialist or anarchist. Again, within the capitalist
orbit, the rebellion against fascist and military dictatorships
(in Spain, in Latin American countries) has a strategy and
goals different from the rebellion in the democratic countries. And one should never forget the one student rebellion

which was instrumental in perpetrating the most despicable mass murder in the contemporary world: the massacre of hundreds of thousands of "communists" in Indonesia. The crime has not yet been punished; it is the only horrible exception from the libertarian, liberating function of student activism.

In the fascist and semifascist countries, the militant students (a minority of the students everywhere) find support among the industrial and agrarian proletariat; in France and Italy, they have been able to obtain precarious (and passing!) aid from powerful leftist parties and unions; in West Germany and in the United States, they meet with the vociferous and often violent hostility of "the people" and of organized labor. Revolutionary in its theory, in its instincts, and in its ultimate goals, the student movement is not a revolutionary force, perhaps not even an avant-garde so long as there are no masses capable and willing to follow, but it is the ferment of hope in the overpowering and stifling capitalist metropoles: it testifies to the truth of the alternative — the real need, and the real possibility of a free society. To be sure, there are the wild ones and the noncommitted, the escapists into all kinds of mysticism, the good fools and the bad fools, and those who don't care what happens; there are the authentic and the organized happenings and nonconformities.

Naturally, the market has invaded this rebellion and made it a business, but it is serious business nevertheless. What matters is not the more or less interesting psychology of the participants nor the often bizarre forms of the protest (which quite frequently make the absurd reasonableness of the Establishment, and the anti-heroic, sensuous images of the alternative more transparent than the most serious argument could do), but that against which

the protest is directed. The demands for a structural reform of the educational system (urgent enough by themselves; we shall come back to them subsequently) seek to counteract the deceptive neutrality and often plainly apologetic teaching; and to provide the student with the conceptual instruments for a solid and thorough critique of the material and intellectual culture. At the same time, they seek to abolish the class character of education. These changes would lead to an extension and development of consciousness which would remove the ideological and technological veil that hides the terrible features of the affluent society.

The development of a true consciousness is still the professional function of the universities. No wonder then that the student opposition meets with the all but pathological hatred on the part of the so-called "community," including large sections of organized labor. To the degree to which the university becomes dependent on the financial and political goodwill of the community and of the government, the struggle for a free and critical education becomes a vital part in the larger struggle for change.

What appears as extraneous "politicalization" of the university by disrupting radicals is today (as it was so often in the past) the "logical," internal dynamic of education: translation of knowledge into reality, of humanistic values into humane conditions of existence. This dynamic, arrested by the pseudo-neutral features of academia, would, for example, be released by the inclusion into the curriculum of courses giving adequate treatment to the great nonconformist movements in civilization and to the critical analysis of contemporary societies. The groundwork for building the bridge between the "ought" and the "is," between theory and practice, is laid within theory itself. Knowledge is transcendent (toward the object world, toward reality) not

only in an epistemological sense — as against repressive
forms of life — it is political. Denial of the right to political
activity in the university perpetuates the separation between theoretical and practical reason and reduces the
effectiveness and the scope of intelligence. The educational demands thus drive the movement beyond the universities, into the streets, the slums, the "community." And
the driving force is the refusal to grow up, to mature, to
perform efficiently and "normally" in and for a society

· which compels the vast majority of the population to
"earn" their living in stupid, inhuman, and unnecessary
jobs,

· which conducts its booming business on the back of
ghettos, slums, and internal and external colonialism,

· which is infested with violence and repression while
demanding obedience and compliance from the victims
of violence and repression,

· which, in order to sustain the profitable productivity
on which its hierarchy depends, utilizes its vast resources
for waste, destruction, and an ever more methodical creation of conformist needs and satisfactions.

To the degree to which the rebellion is directed against
a functioning, prosperous, "democratic" society, it is a
moral rebellion, against the hypocritical, aggressive values
and goals, against the blasphemous religion of this society,
against everything it takes seriously, everything it professes
while violating what it professes.

The "unorthodox" character of this opposition, which does
not have the traditional class basis, and which is at the same
time a political, instinctual, and moral rebellion, shapes
the strategy and scope of the rebellion. It extends to the
entire organization of the existing liberal-parliamentary

democracy. Among the New Left, a strong revulsion against traditional politics prevails: against that whole network of parties, committees, and pressure groups on all levels; against working within this network and with its methods. This entire sphere and atmosphere, with all its power, is invalidated; nothing that any of these politicians, representatives, or candidates declares is of any relevance to the rebels; they cannot take it seriously although they know very well that it may mean to them getting beaten, going to jail, losing a job. They are not professional martyrs: they prefer not to be beaten, not to go to jail, not to lose their job. But for them, this is not a question of choice; the protest and refusal are parts of their metabolism, and they extend to the power structure as a whole. The democratic process organized by this structure is discredited to such an extent that no part of it can be extracted which is not contaminated. Moreover, using this process would divert energy to snail-paced movements. For example, electioneering with the aim of significantly changing the composition of the U.S. Congress might take a hundred years, judging by the present rate of progress, and assuming that the effort of political radicalization continues unchecked. And the performance of the courts, from the lowest to the highest, does not mitigate the distrust in the given democratic-constitutional setup. Under these circumstances, to work for the improvement of the existing democracy easily appears as indefinitely delaying attainment of the goal of creating a free society.

Thus, in some sectors of the opposition, the radical protest tends to become antinomian, anarchistic, and even non-political. Here is another reason why the rebellion often takes on the weird and clownish forms which get on the nerves of the Establishment. In the face of the gruesomely serious totality of institutionalized politics, satire, irony, and laughing provocation become a necessary dimension of the new politics. The contempt for the deadly *esprit de sérieux* which permeates the talkings and doings of the professional and semiprofessional politicians appears as contempt for the values which they profess while destroying them. The rebels revive the desperate laughter and the cynical defiance of the fool as means for demasking the deeds of the serious ones who govern the whole.

This alienation of the radical opposition from the existing democratic process and institutions suggests a thorough reexamination of democracy ("bourgeois" democracy, representative government) and of their role in the transition from capitalism to socialism or, generally, from an unfree to a free society. By and large, Marxian theory has a positive evaluation of the role of bourgeois democracy in this transition — up to the stage of the revolution itself. By virtue of its commitment (however limited in practice) to civil rights and liberties, bourgeois democracy provides the most favorable ground for the development and organization of dissent. This is still true, but the forces which vitiate the "protective" features within the democratic framework itself are gaining momentum. The mass democracy developed by monopoly capitalism has shaped the rights and liberties which it grants in its own image and interest; the majority of the people is the majority of their masters; deviations are easily "contained"; and concentrated power can afford to tolerate (perhaps even defend) radical dissent as long as the latter complies with the established rules and manners (and even a little beyond it). The opposition is thus sucked into the very world which it opposes — and by the very mechanisms which allow its development and organization; the opposition without a mass basis is frustrated in its efforts to obtain such a mass basis. Under these circumstances, working according to the rules and methods of democratic legality appears as surrender to the prevailing power structure. And yet, it would be fatal to abandon the defense of civil rights and liberties within the established framework. But as monopoly capitalism is compelled to extend and fortify its dominion at home and abroad, the democratic struggle will come into increasing conflict with the existing democratic institutions: with its built-in barriers and conservative dynamic.

The semi-democratic process works of necessity against radical change because it produces and sustains a popular majority whose opinion is generated by the dominant interests in the *status quo*. As long as this condition prevails, it makes sense to say that the general will is always wrong — wrong inasmuch as it objectively counteracts the possible transformation of society into more humane ways of life. To be sure, the method of persuasion is still open to the minority, but it is fatally reduced by the fact that the leftist minority does not possess the large funds required for equal access to the mass media which speak day and night for the dominant interests — with those wholesome interludes in favor of the opposition that buttress the illusory faith in prevailing equality and fair play. And yet, without the continuous effort of persuasion, of reducing, one by one, the hostile majority, the prospects of the opposition would be still darker than they are.

Dialectics of democracy: if democracy means self-government of free people, with justice for all, then the realization of democracy would presuppose abolition of the existing pseudo-democracy. In the dynamic of corporate capitalism, the fight for democracy thus tends to assume anti-democratic forms, and to the extent to which the democratic decisions are made in "parliaments" on all levels, the opposition will tend to become extraparliamentary. The movement to extend constitutionally professed rights and liberties to the daily life of the oppressed minorities, even the movement to preserve existing rights and liberties, will become "subversive" to the degree to which it will meet the stiffening resistance of the majority against an "exaggerated" interpretation and application of equality and justice.

An opposition which is directed, not against a particular form of government or against particular conditions within a society, but against a given social system as a whole, cannot remain legal and lawful because it is the established legality and the established law which it opposes. The fact that the democratic process provides for the redress of grievances and for legal and lawful changes does not alter the illegality inherent in an opposition to an institutionalized democracy which halts the process of change at the stage where it would destroy the existing system. By virtue of this built-in stabilizer or "governor," capitalist mass-democracy is perhaps to a higher degree self-perpetuating than any other form of government or society; and the more so the more it rests, not on terror and scarcity, but on efficiency and wealth, and on the majority will of the underlying and administered population. This new situation has direct bearing on the old question as to the right of resistance. Can we say that it is the established system rather than the resistance to it which is in need of justification? Such seems to be the implication of the social contract theories which consider civil society dissolved when, in its existing form, it no longer fulfills the functions for which it was set up, namely, as a system of socially necessary and productive repression. Theoretically, these functions were

determined by the philosophers: the realistically minded
defined the "end of government" as the protection of property, trade, and commerce; the idealists spoke of the realization of Reason, Justice, Freedom (without altogether neg-
lecting or even minimizing the more material and economic
aspects). In both schools, judgment as to whether a government actually fulfilled these "ends," and the criteria
for judging, were usually limited to the particular nation-
state (or type of nation-state) which the respective phi-
losopher had in mind: that the security, growth, and
freedom of the one nation-state involved the insecurity, destruction, or oppression of another did not invalidate the
definition, nor did an established government lose its claim
for obedience when the protection of property and the
realization of reason left large parts of the population in
poverty and servitude.

In the contemporary period, the questions as to the "end
of government" have subsided. It seems that the continued
functioning of the society is sufficient justification for its
legality and its claim for obedience, and "functioning"
seems defined rather negatively as absence of civil war,
massive disorder, economic collapse. Otherwise anything
goes: military dictatorship, plutocracy, government by
gangs and rackets. Genocide, war crimes, crimes against
humanity are not effective arguments against a government
which protects property, trade, and commerce at home
while it perpetrates its destructive policy abroad. And indeed, there is no enforceable law that could deprive such
a constitutional government of its legitimacy and legality.
But this means that there is no (enforceable) law other
than that which serves the *status quo*, and that those who
refuse such service are *eo ipso* outside the realm of law even
before they come into actual conflict with the law.

The absurd situation: the established democracy still provides the only legitimate framework for change and must therefore be defended against all attempts on the Right and the Center to restrict this framework, but at the same time, preservation of the established democracy preserves the *status quo* and the containment of change. Another aspect of the same ambiguity: radical change depends on a mass basis, but every step in the struggle for radical change isolates the opposition from the masses and provokes intensified repression: mobilization of institutionalized violence against the opposition, thus further diminishing the prospects for radical change. After the electoral triumph of the reaction over the Left in the aftermath of the French student rebellion, *Humanité* wrote (according to *The Los Angeles Times*, June 25, 1968): "every barricade, every car burned gave tens of thousands of votes to the Gaullist party." This is perfectly correct — as perfectly correct as the corollary proposition that without the barricades and car burnings the ruling powers would be safer and stronger, and the opposition, absorbed and restricted by the parliamentary game, would further emasculate and pacify the masses on whom the change depends. The conclusion? The radical opposition inevitably faces defeat of its direct, extraparliamentary action, of uncivil disobedience, and there are situations in which it must take the risk of such defeat — if, in doing so, it can consolidate its strength and expose the destructive character of civil obedience to a reactionary regime.

For it is precisely the objective, historical function of the democratic system of corporate capitalism to use the Law and Order of bourgeois liberalism as a counterrevolutionary force, thus imposing upon the radical opposition the necessity of direct action and uncivil disobedience, while con-

fronting the opposition with its vastly superior strength.
Under these circumstances, direct action and uncivil disobedience become for the rebels integral parts of the transformation of the indirect democracy of corporate capitalism
into a direct democracy [3] in which elections and representation no longer serve as institutions of domination. As against
the latter, direct action becomes a means of democratiza-
tion, of change even within the established system. All its
power could not silence the student opposition (weakest and
most diffused of all historical oppositions); and there is
good reason to believe that it was, not the parliamentary
and the Gallup poll opinion, but rather the students and the
resistance which enforced the change in the attitude of
the government toward the war in Vietnam. And it was the
uncivil disobedience of the students of Paris which sud-
denly broke through the memory repression of organized
labor and recalled, for a very short moment, the historical
power of the general strike and the factory occupation, of
the red flag and the International.

The alternative is, not democratic evolution versus radical action, but rationalization of the *status quo* versus
change. As long as a social system reproduces, by indoc-
trination and integration, a self-perpetuating conservative
majority, the majority reproduces the system itself — open
to changes within, but not beyond, its institutional framework. Consequently, the struggle for changes beyond the
system becomes, by virtue of its own dynamic, undemo-
cratic in the terms of the system, and counterviolence is

[3] "Direct democracy": in modern mass society, democracy, no matter
in what form, is not conceivable without a system of representation. Direct democracy would assure, on all levels, genuinely free selection and
election of candidates, revocability at the discretion of the constituencies,
and uncensored education and information. Again, such democracy presupposes equal and universal education for autonomy.

from the beginning inherent in this dynamic. Thus the radical is guilty — either of surrendering to the power of the *status quo*, or of violating the Law and Order of the *status quo*.

But who has the right to set himself up as judge of an established society, who other than the legally constituted agencies or agents, and the majority of the people? Other than these, it could only be a self-appointed elite, or leaders who would arrogate to themselves such judgment. Indeed, if the alternative were between democracy and dictatorship (no matter how "benevolent"), the answer would be noncontroversial: democracy is preferable. However, this democracy does not exist, and the government is factually exercised by a network of pressure groups and "machines," vested interests represented by and working on and through the democratic institutions. These are not derived from a sovereign people. The representation is representative of the will shaped by the ruling minorities. Consequently, if the alternative is rule by an elite, it would only mean replacement of the present ruling elite by another; and if this other should be the dreaded intellectual elite, it may not be less qualified and less threatening than the prevailing one. True, such government, initially, would not have the endorsement of the majority "inherited" from the previous government — but once the chain of the past governments is broken, the majority would be in a state of flux, and, released from the past management, free to judge the new government in terms of the new common interest. To be sure, this has never been the course of a revolution, but it is equally true that never before has a revolution occurred which had at its disposal the present achievements of productivity and technical progress. Of course, they could be effectively used for imposing another set of repressive controls, but our entire discussion was based on the proposition that the revolution would be liberating only if it were carried by the non-repressive forces stirring in the existing society. The proposition is no more — and no less — than a hope. Prior to its realization, it is indeed only the individual, the individuals, who can judge, with no other legitimation than their consciousness and conscience. But these individuals are more and other than private persons with their particular contingent preferences and interests. Their judgment transcends their subjectivity to the degree to which it is based on independent thought and information, on a rational analysis and evaluation of their society. The existence of a majority of individuals capable of such rationality has been the assumption on which democratic theory has been based. If the established majority is not composed of such individuals, it does not think, will, and act as sovereign people.

The old story: right against right — the positive, codified, enforceable right of the existing society against the negative, unwritten, unenforceable right of transcendence which is part of the very existence of man in history: the right to insist on a less compromised, less guilty, less exploited humanity. The two rights must come into violent conflict as long as the established society depends, for its functioning, on exploitation and guilt. The opposition cannot change this state of affairs by the very means which protect and sustain the state of affairs. Beyond it, there are only the ideal and the offense, and those who claim, for their offending action, a right have to answer for their action before the tribunal of the existing society. For neither conscience nor commitment to an ideal can legalize the subversion of an established order which defines order, or even legalize disturbance of the peace which is the peace of the

established order. To the latter alone belongs the lawful
right to abrogate peace and to organize the killing and
beating. In the established vocabulary, "violence" is a term
which one does not apply to the action of the police, the
National Guard, the Marshals, the Marines, the bombers.
The "bad" words are a priori reserved for the Enemy, and
their meaning is defined and validated by the actions of
the Enemy regardless of their motivation and goal. No matter how "good" the end, it does not justify the illegal means.[4]

[4] A frightful example of the language of counter-sense — destruction
not only of the meaning of words but also of the very idea of humanity —
is provided by a report in *The New York Times* (September 5, 1967)
which contains the following passages:

> County Judge Christ Seraphim sat with his golden retriever, Holly,
> on the porch of his Spanish-style house on a pleasant East Side street
> [in Milwaukee] this afternoon and made some acerbic comments on
> 1,000 civil rights demonstrators who jived and strutted past his front
> lawn. . . .
> "I think they are disturbing the peace, don't you?" he asked, look-
> ing at the marchers today. "They are loud and boisterous, are they
> not? I can't enjoy the peace and tranquillity of my home, a home I
> paid a lot for."
> As for the Rev. James E. Groppi, the white Roman Catholic priest
> who commands the marchers, Judge Seraphim snapped: "He is a
> criminal, a convicted criminal, convicted twice by a jury for disorderly
> conduct."
> The demonstrators finally moved out of earshot, and Judge Seraphim
> resumed, with a grateful sigh, his reading of "A History of the Jews"
> by Abram Leon Sacher, president of Brandeis University, but soon
> the marchers returned.
> "These people," said Judge Seraphim, this time referring to his
> book, "were baked in ovens. But they maintained their dignity to the
> end. They didn't do much marching. They are the most law-abiding
> people in the world."

The epitome of Law and Order: men are law-abiding if they go
to the ovens and get baked without "much marching," while those who
march in order to protest and to prevent a possible repetition of the concentration camps are "disturbing the peace" and "criminal" is the priest

The proposition "the end justifies the means" is indeed, as a general statement, intolerable — but so is, as a general statement, its negation. In radical political practice, the end belongs to a world different from and contrary to the established universe of discourse and behavior. But the means belong to the latter and are judged by the latter, on its own terms, the very terms which the end invalidates. For example, assuming an action aims at stopping crimes against humanity committed in the professed national interest; and the means to attain this goal are acts of organized civil disobedience. In accord with established law and order not the crimes but the attempt to stop them is condemned and punished as a crime; thus it is judged by the very standards which the action indicts. The existing society defines the transcending action on its, society's, own terms — a self-validating procedure, entirely legitimate, even necessary for this society: one of the most effective rights of the Sovereign is the right to establish enforceable definitions of words.[5]

Political linguistics: armor of the Establishment. If the radical opposition develops its own language, it protests spontaneously, subconsciously, against one of the most ef-

---

who leads the protest. And the counter-sense triumphs in the very name of the Judge: Christ Seraphim.

[5] "Nous contestons une culture qui donne la suprématie au langage-parlé. Ce langage élaboré par la classe bourgeoise est un signe d'appartenance à cette classe. Mais ce langage qui est le fait d'une minorité d'individus s'impose à tous comme le seul mode de communication valable; . . . Le langage n'est pas seulement un moyen de communication, c'est aussi et surtout un mode d'appréhension de la réalité, celui tout formel et tout intellectuel que peut se permettre une classe détachée par ses privilèges économiques des conflits et des contradictions de la vie sociale": (Extrait de *Majuscule*, organe de liaison de la faculté de Lyon, 29 mai 1968. *Quelle université? Quelle société?*, *loc. cit.*, pp. 45–46.)

fective "secret weapons" of domination and defamation. The language of the prevailing Law and Order, validated by the courts and by the police, is not only the voice but also the deed of suppression.[6] This language not only defines and condemns the Enemy, it also *creates* him; and this creation is not the Enemy as he really is but rather as he must be in order to perform his function for the Establishment. The end now does justify the means: actions cease to be crimes if they serve to preserve and extend the

[6] Awareness of this fact and its implications is rarely found in the respectable press. An amazing exception is an article by David S. Broder in *The Los Angeles Times* of October 1, 1968. It contains the following passages:

The systematic stripping of meaning and substance from words is a form of subversion not covered by statute. Nor are politicians the only guilty parties. A nation that had grown accustomed to hearing reports of heavy fighting in the "demilitarized zone" or of persons being injured in a "non-violent demonstration" was already well on its way to losing a grip on its sanity.

Rhetorical excesses are accepted as part of any campaign, but this year the candidates have been exceptionally profligate in wasting the resources of the language. The words "law" and "order," and "peace," for example, are fundamental to the vocabulary of citizens of a free country. Yet the meaning has been drained from these words as higher charges of emotion have been added. . . .

But the American experiment in self-government was launched in a society where certain abstract concepts were well-understood. If they had not been part of every man's vocabulary, the system of self-government could never have been attempted.

Jefferson could expect to be understood when he wrote: "We hold these truths to be self-evident; that all men are created equal; that they are endowed by their creator with certain inalienable rights; that among these are life, liberty and the pursuit of happiness."

The concepts in that statement cannot be visualized; they must be defined.

And when words lose their meaning, when the medium overwhelms the message, a system of government like ours may no longer be operable.

"Free World." Conversely, what the Enemy does, is evil; what he says — propaganda. This a priori linguistic defamation hits first the Enemy abroad: the defense of his own land, his own hut, his own naked life is a crime, the supreme crime which deserves the supreme punishment. Long before the special and not-so-special forces are physically trained to kill, burn, and interrogate, their minds and bodies are already desensitized to see and hear and smell in the Other not a human being but a beast — a beast however, which is subject to all-out punishment. The linguistic pattern constantly repeats itself: In Vietnam, "typical criminal communist violence" is perpetrated against American "strategic operations"; the Reds have the impertinence to "launch a sneak attack" (presumably they are supposed to announce it beforehand and to deploy in the open); they are "evading a death trap" (presumably they should have stayed in). The Viet Cong attack American barracks "in the dead of night" and kill American boys (presumably, Americans only attack in broad daylight, don't disturb the sleep of the enemy, and don't kill Vietnamese boys). The massacre of hundreds of thousands of communists (in Indonesia) is called "impressive" — a comparable "killing rate" suffered by the other side would hardly have been honored with such an adjective. To the Chinese, the presence of American troops in East Asia is a threat to their "ideology," while presumably the presence of Chinese troops in Central or South America would be a real, and not only an ideological, threat to the United States.

This linguistic universe, which incorporates the Enemy (as *Untermensch*) into the routine of everyday speech, can be transcended only in action. For violence is built into the very structure of this society: as the accumulated aggressiveness which drives the business of life in all branches of

corporate capitalism, as the legal aggression on the highways, and as the national aggression abroad which seems
to become more brutal the more it takes as its victims the
wretched of the earth — those who have not yet been civilized by the capital of the Free World. In the mobilization
of this aggressiveness, ancient psychical forces are activated
to serve the economic-political needs of the system: the
Enemy are those who are unclean, infested; they are ani-
mals rather than humans; they are contagious (the domino
theory!) and threaten the clean, anesthetized, healthy free
world.[7] They must be liquidated, smoked out, and burned
out like venom; their infested jungles too must be burned
out and cleared for freedom and democracy. The Enemy
already has its "fifth column" inside the clean world: the
Commies and the Hippies and their like with the long hair
and the beards and the dirty pants — those who are promis-
cuous and take liberties which are denied to the clean and
orderly who remain clean and orderly even when they kill
and bomb and burn. Never perhaps since the Middle Ages
has accumulated repression erupted on such global scale
in organized aggression against those outside the repressive system — "outsiders" within and without.

In the face of the scope and intensity of this sanctioned
aggression, the traditional distinction between legitimate
and illegitimate violence becomes questionable. If legitimate violence includes, in the daily routine of "pacification" and "liberation," wholesale burning, poisoning,
bombing, the actions of the radical opposition, no matter
how illegitimate, can hardly be called by the same name:

[7] See "The Americans in Vietnam" (anonymous) in *Alternatives,* University of California, San Diego, Fall 1966; originally published in Ger-
man in *Das Argument,* No. 36, Berlin, 1966; in French in *Les Temps
Modernes,* January 1966.

violence. Can there be any meaningful comparison, in magnitude and criminality, between the unlawful acts committed by the rebels in the ghettos, on the campuses, on the city streets on the one side, and the deeds perpetrated by the forces of order in Vietnam, in Bolivia, in Indonesia, in Guatemala, on the other? Can one meaningfully call it an offense when demonstrators disrupt the business of the university, the draft board, the supermarket, the flow of traffic, to protest against the far more efficient disruption of the business of life of untold numbers of human beings by the armed forces of law and order? Here too, the brute reality requires a redefinition of terms: the established vocabulary discriminates a priori against the opposition — it protects the Establishment.

"Law and Order": these words have always had an ominous sound; the entire necessity and the entire horror of legitimate force are condensed, and sanctioned, in this phrase. There can be no human association without law and order, enforceable law and order, but there are degrees of good and evil in human associations — measured in terms of the legitimate, organized violence required to protect the established society against the poor, the oppressed, the insane: the victims of its well-being. Over and above their legitimacy in constitutional terms, the extent to which established law and order can legitimately demand (and command) obedience and compliance largely depends (or ought to depend) on the extent to which this law and this order obey and comply with their own standards and values. These may first be ideological (like the ideas of liberty, equality, fraternity advanced by the revolutionary bourgeoisie), but the ideology can become a material political force in the armor of the opposition as these values are betrayed, compromised, denied in the social reality.

Then the betrayed promises are, as it were, "taken over" by the opposition, and with them the claim for legitimacy. In this situation, law and order become something to be established as *against* the established law and order: the existing society has become illegitimate, unlawful: it has invalidated its own law. Such has been the dynamic of the historical revolutions; it is hard to see how it can be arrested indefinitely.

IV. Solidarity

THE PRECEDING ATTEMPT to analyze the present opposition to the society organized by corporate capitalism was focused on the striking contrast between the radical and total character of the rebellion on the one hand, and the absence of a class basis for this radicalism on the other. This situation gives all efforts to evaluate and even discuss the prospects for radical change in the domain of corporate capitalism their abstract, academic, unreal character. The search for specific historical agents of revolutionary change in the advanced capitalist countries is indeed meaningless. Revolutionary forces emerge in the process of change itself; the translation of the potential into the actual is the work of political practice. And just as little as critical theory can political practice orient itself on a concept of revolution which belongs to the nineteenth and early twentieth century, and which is still valid in large areas of the Third World. This concept envisages the "seizure of power" in the course of a mass upheaval, led by a revolutionary party acting as the avant-garde of a revolutionary class and setting up a new central power which would initiate the basic social changes. Even in industrial countries where a strong Marxist party has organized the exploited masses, strategy is no longer guided by this notion — witness the long-range Communist policy of "popular fronts." And the concept is altogether inapplicable to those countries in which the integration of the working class is the result of structural economic-politicial processes (sustained high productivity; large markets; neo-colonialism; administered democracy) and where the masses themselves are forces of conservatism and stabilization. It is the very power of this society which contains new modes and dimensions of radical change.

The dynamic of this society has long since passed the stage where it could grow on its own resources, its own market, and on normal trade with other areas. It has grown into an imperialist power which, through economic and technical penetration and outright military intervention, has transformed large parts of the Third World into dependencies. Its policy is distinguished from classical imperialism of the preceding period by effective use of economic and technical conquests on the one hand, and by the political-strategic character of intervention on the other: the requirements of the global fight against communism supersede those of profitable investments. In any case, by virtue of the evolution of imperialism, the developments in the Third World pertain to the dynamic of the First World, and the forces of change in the former are not extraneous to the latter; the "external proletariat" is a basic factor of potential change within the dominion of corporate capitalism. Here is the coincidence of the historical factors of revolution: this predominantly agrarian proletariat endures the dual oppression exercised by the indigenous ruling classes and those of the foreign metropoles. A liberal bourgeoisie which would ally itself with the poor and lead their struggle does not exist. Kept in abject material and mental privation, they depend on a militant leadership.

Since the vast majority outside the cities is unable to mount any concerted economic and political action which would threaten the existing society, the struggle for liberation will be a predominantly military one, carried out with the support of the local population, and exploiting the advantages of a terrain which impedes traditional methods of suppression. These circumstances, of necessity, make for guerrilla warfare. It is the great chance, and at the same time the terrible danger, for the forces of liberation. The powers that be will not tolerate a repetition of the Cuban example; they will employ ever more effective means and weapons of suppression, and the indigenous dictatorships will be strengthened with the ever more active aid from the imperialist metropoles. It would be romanticism to underrate the strength of this deadly alliance and its resolution to contain subversion. It seems that not the features of the terrain, nor the unimaginable resistance of the men and women of Vietnam, nor considerations of "world opinion," but fear of the other nuclear powers has so far prevented the use of nuclear or seminuclear weapons against a whole people and a whole country.

Under these circumstances, the preconditions for the liberation and development of the Third World must emerge in the advanced capitalist countries. Only the internal weakening of the superpower can finally stop the financing and equipping of suppression in the backward countries. The National Liberation Fronts threaten the life line of imperialism; they are not only a material but also an ideological catalyst of change. The Cuban revolution and the Viet Cong have demonstrated: it can be done; there is a morality, a humanity, a will, and a faith which can resist and deter the gigantic technical and economic force of capitalist expansion. More than the "socialist humanism" of the early Marx, this violent solidarity in defense, this elemental socialism in action, has given form and substance to the radicalism of the New Left; in this ideological respect too, the external revolution has become an essential part of the opposition within the capitalist metropoles. However, the exemplary force, the ideological power of the external revolution, can come to fruition only if the internal structure and cohesion of the capitalist system begin to disintegrate. The chain of exploitation must break at its strongest link.

Corporate capitalism is not immune against economic crisis. The huge "defense" sector of the economy not only places an increasingly heavy burden on the taxpayer, it also is largely responsible for the narrowing margin of profit. The growing opposition against the war in Vietnam points up the necessity of a thorough conversion of the economy, risking the danger of rising unemployment, which is a by-product of technical progress in automation. The "peaceful" creation of additional outlets for the productivity of the metropoles would meet with the intensified resistance in the Third World, and with the contesting and competitive strength of the Soviet orbit. The absorption of unemployment and the maintenance of an adequate rate of profit would thus require the stimulation of demand on an ever larger scale, thereby stimulating the rat race of the competitive struggle for existence through the multiplication of waste, planned obsolescence, parasitic and stupid jobs and services. The higher standard of living, propelled by the growing parasitic sector of the economy, would drive wage demands toward capital's point of no return. But the structural tendencies which determine the development of corporate capitalism do not justify the assumption that aggravated class struggles would terminate in a socialist revolution through organized political action. To be sure, even the most advanced capitalist welfare state remains a class society and therefore a state of conflicting class interests. However, prior to the disintegration of the state power, the apparatus and the suppressive force of the system would keep the class struggle within the capitalist framework. The translation of the economic into the radical political struggle would be the consequence rather than the cause of change. The change itself could then occur in a general, unstructured, unorganized, and diffused process of disintegration. This process may be sparked by a crisis of the system which would activate the resistance not only against the political but also against the mental repression imposed by the society. Its insane features, expression of the ever more blatant contradiction between the available resources for liberation and their use for the perpetuation of servitude, would undermine the daily routine, the repressive conformity, and rationality required for the continued functioning of the society.

The dissolution of social morality may manifest itself in a collapse of work discipline, slowdown, spread of disobedience to rules and regulations, wildcat strikes, boycotts, sabotage, gratuitous acts of noncompliance. The violence built into the system of repression may get out of control, or necessitate ever more totalitarian controls.

Even the most totalitarian technocratic-political administration depends, for its functioning, on what is usually called the "moral fiber": a (relatively) "positive" attitude among the underlying population toward the usefulness of their work and toward the necessity of the repressions exacted by the social organization of work. A society depends on the relatively stable and calculable sanity of the people, sanity defined as the regular, socially coordinated functioning of mind and body — especially at work, in the shops and offices, but also at leisure and fun. Moreover, a society also demands to a considerable extent, belief in one's beliefs (which is part of the required sanity); belief in the operative value of society's values. Operationalism is indeed an indispensable supplement to want and fear as forces of cohesion.

Now it is the strength of this moral fiber, of the operational values (quite apart from their ideational validity), which is likely to wear off under the impact of the growing contradictions within the society. The result would be a spread, not only of discontent and mental sickness, but also of inefficiency, resistance to work, refusal to perform, negligence, indifference — factors of dysfunction which would hit a highly centralized and coordinated apparatus, where breakdown at one point may easily affect large sections of the whole. To be sure, these are subjective factors, but they may assume material force in conjunction with the objective economic and political strains to which the system will be exposed on a global scale. Then, and only then, that political climate would prevail which could provide a mass basis for the new forms of organization required for directing the struggle.

We have indicated the tendencies which threaten the stability of the imperialist society and emphasized the extent to which the liberation movements in the Third World affect the prospective development of this society. It is to an even greater extent affected by the dynamic of "peaceful coexistence" with the old socialist societies, the Soviet orbit. In important aspects, this coexistence has contributed to the stabilization of capitalism: "world communism" has been the Enemy who would have to be invented if he did not exist — the Enemy whose strength justified the "defense economy" and the mobilization of the people in the national interest. Moreover, as the common Enemy of *all* capitalism, communism promoted the organization of a common interest superseding the intercapitalist differences and conflicts. Last but not least, the opposition within the advanced capitalist countries has been seriously weakened by the repressive Stalinist development of socialism, which made socialism not exactly an attractive alternative to capitalism.

More recently, the break in the unity of the communist orbit, the triumph of the Cuban revolution, Vietnam, and the "cultural revolution" in China have changed this picture. The possibility of constructing socialism on a truly popular base, without the Stalinist bureaucratization and the danger of a nuclear war as the imperialist answer to the emergence of this kind of socialist power, has led to some sort of common interest between the Soviet Union on the one side and the United States on the other.

In a sense, this is indeed the community of interests of the "haves" against the "have nots," of the Old against the New. The "collaborationist" policy of the Soviet Union necessitates the pursuance of power politics which increasingly reduces the prospect that Soviet society, by virtue of its basic institutions alone (abolition of private ownership and control of the means of production: planned economy) is still capable of making the transition to a free society. And yet, the very dynamic of imperialist expansion places the Soviet Union in the other camp: would the effective resistance in Vietnam, and the protection of Cuba be possible without Soviet aid?

However, while we reject the unqualified convergence thesis, according to which — at least at present — the assimilation of interests prevails upon the conflict between capitalism and Soviet socialism, we cannot minimize the

essential difference between the latter and the new historical efforts to construct socialism by developing and creating
a genuine solidarity between the leadership and the liberated victims of exploitation. The actual may considerably
deviate from the ideal, the fact remains that, for a whole
generation, "freedom," "socialism," and "liberation" are
inseparable from Fidel and Ché and the guerrillas — not
because their revolutionary struggle could furnish the
model for the struggle in the metropoles, but because they
have recaptured the truth of these ideas, in the day-to-day
fight of men and women for a life as human beings: for a
new life.

What kind of life? We are still confronted with the demand to state the "concrete alternative." The demand is
meaningless if it asks for a blueprint of the specific institutions and relationships which would be those of the new
society: they cannot be determined a priori; they will develop, in trial and error, as the new society develops. If we
could form a concrete concept of the alternative today, it
would not be that of an alternative; the possibilities of the
new society are sufficiently "abstract," i.e., removed from
and incongruous with the established universe to defy any
attempt to identify them in terms of this universe. However,
the question cannot be brushed aside by saying that what
matters today is the destruction of the old, of the powers
that be, making way for the emergence of the new. Such an
answer neglects the essential fact that the old is not simply
bad, that it delivers the goods, and that people have a real
stake in it. There can be societies which are much worse —
there are such societies today. The system of corporate
capitalism has the right to insist that those who work for its
replacement justify their action.

But the demand to state the concrete alternatives is justi-

fied for yet another reason. Negative thinking draws whatever force it may have from its empirical basis: the actual
human condition in the given society, and the "given" possibilities to transcend this condition, to enlarge the realm of
freedom. In this sense, negative thinking is by virtue of its
own internal concepts "positive": oriented toward, and
comprehending a future which is "contained" in the present. And in this containment (which is an important aspect
of the general containment policy pursued by the established societies), the future appears as possible liberation.
It is not the only alternative: the advent of a long period of
"civilized" barbarism, with or without the nuclear destruction, is equally contained in the present. Negative thinking,
and the praxis guided by it, is the positive and positing
effort to prevent this utter negativity.

The concept of the primary, initial institutions of liberation is familiar enough and concrete enough: collective
ownership, collective control and planning of the means of
production and distribution. This is the foundation, a necessary but not sufficient condition for the alternative: it would
make possible the usage of all available resources for the
abolition of poverty, which is the prerequisite for the turn
from quantity into quality: the creation of a reality in
accordance with the new sensitivity and the new consciousness. This goal implies rejection of those policies of
reconstruction, no matter how revolutionary, which are
bound to perpetuate (or to introduce) the pattern of the
unfree societies and their needs. Such false policy is perhaps
best summed up in the formula "to catch up with, and to
overtake the productivity level of the advanced capitalist
countries." What is wrong with this formula is not the
emphasis on the rapid improvement of the material conditions but on the model guiding their improvement. The

model denies the alternative, the qualitative difference. The latter is not, and cannot be, the result of the fastest possible attainment of capitalist productivity, but rather the development of new modes and ends of production — "new" not only (and perhaps not at all) with respect to technical innovations and production relations, but with respect to the different human needs and the different human relationships in working for the satisfaction of these needs. These new relationships would be the result of a "biological" *solidarity* in work and purpose, expressive of a true harmony between social and individual needs and goals, between recognized necessity and free development — the exact opposite of the administered and enforced harmony organized in the advanced capitalist (and socialist?) countries. It is the image of this solidarity as elemental, instinctual, creative force which the young radicals see in Cuba, in the guerrillas, in the Chinese cultural revolution.

Solidarity and cooperation: not all their forms are liberating. Fascism and militarism have developed a deadly efficient solidarity. Socialist solidarity is autonomy: self-determination begins at home — and that is with every I, and the We whom the I chooses. And this end must indeed appear in the means to attain it, that is to say, in the strategy of those who, within the existing society, work for the new one. If the socialist relationships of production are to be a new way of life, a new Form of life, then their existential quality must show forth, anticipated and demonstrated, in the fight for their realization. Exploitation in all its forms must have disappeared from this fight: from the work relationships among the fighters as well as from their individual relationships. Understanding, tenderness toward each other, the instinctual consciousness of that which is evil, false, the heritage of oppression, would then testify to the authenticity of the rebellion. In short, the economic, political, and cultural features of a classless society must have become the basic needs of those who fight for it. This ingression of the future into the present, this depth dimension of the rebellion accounts, in the last analysis, for the incompatibility with the traditional forms of the political struggle. The new radicalism militates against the centralized bureaucratic communist as well as against the semi-democratic liberal organization. There is a strong element of spontaneity, even anarchism, in this rebellion, expression of the new sensibility, sensitivity against domination: the feeling, the awareness, that the joy of freedom and the need to be free must precede liberation. Therefore the aversion against preestablished Leaders, apparatchiks of all sorts, politicians no matter how leftist. The initiative shifts to small groups, widely diffused, with a high degree of autonomy, mobility, flexibility.

To be sure, within the repressive society, and against its ubiquitous apparatus, spontaneity by itself cannot possibly be a radical and revolutionary force. It can become such a force only as the result of enlightenment, education, political practice — in this sense indeed, as a result of organization. The anarchic element is an essential factor in the struggle against domination: preserved but disciplined in the preparatory political action, it will be freed and *aufgehoben* in the goals of the struggle. Released for the construction of the initial revolutionary institutions, the antirepressive sensibility, allergic to domination, would militate against the prolongation of the "First Phase," that is, the authoritarian bureaucratic development of the productive forces. The new society could then reach relatively fast the level at which poverty could be abolished (this level could be considerably lower than that of advanced capitalist productivity, which is geared to obscene affluence and waste). Then the development could tend toward a sensuous culture, tangibly contrasting with the gray-on-gray culture of the socialist societies of Eastern Europe. Production would be redirected in defiance of all the rationality of the Performance Principle; socially necessary labor would be diverted to the construction of an aesthetic rather than repressive environment, to parks and gardens rather than highways and parking lots, to the creation of areas of withdrawal rather than massive fun and relaxation. Such redistribution of socially necessary labor (time), incompatible with any society governed by the Profit and Performance Principle, would gradually alter society in all its dimensions — it would mean the ascent of the Aesthetic Principle as Form of the Reality Principle: a culture of receptivity based on the achievements of industrial civilization and initiating the end of its self-propelling productivity.

Not regression to a previous stage of civilization, but return to an imaginary *temps perdu* in the real life of mankind: progress to a stage of civilization where man has learned to ask for the sake of whom or of what he organizes his society; the stage where he checks and perhaps even halts his incessant struggle for existence on an enlarged scale, surveys what has been achieved through centuries of misery and hecatombs of victims, and decides that it is enough, and that it is time to enjoy what he has and what can be reproduced and refined with a minimum of alienated labor: not the arrest or reduction of technical progress, but the elimination of those of its features which perpetuate man's subjection to the apparatus and the intensification of the struggle for existence — to work harder in order to get more of the merchandise that has to be sold. In other words, electrification indeed, and all technical devices which alleviate and protect life, all the mechanization which frees human energy and time, all the standardization which does away with spurious and parasitarian "personalized" services rather than multiplying them and the gadgets and tokens of exploitative affluence. In terms of the latter (and only in terms of the latter), this would certainly be a regression — but freedom from the rule of merchandise over man is a precondition of freedom.

The construction of a free society would create new incentives for work. In the exploitative societies, the so-called work instinct is mainly the (more or less effectively) introjected necessity to perform productively in order to earn a living. But the life instincts themselves strive for the unification and enhancement of life; in nonrepressive sublimation they would provide the libidinal energy for work on the development of a reality which no longer demands the exploitative repression of the Pleasure Principle. The "incentives" would then be built into the instinctual structure of men. Their sensibility would register, as biological reactions, the difference between the ugly and the beautiful, between calm and noise, tenderness and brutality, intelligence and stupidity, joy and fun, and it would correlate this distinction with that between freedom and servitude. Freud's last theoretical conception recognizes the erotic instincts as work instincts — work for the creation of a sensuous environment. The social expression of the liberated work instinct is *cooperation*, which, grounded in solidarity, directs the organization of the realm of necessity and the development of the realm of freedom. And there is an answer to the question which troubles the minds of so many men of good will: what are the people in a free society going to do? The answer which, I believe, strikes at the heart of the matter was given by a young black girl. She said: for the first time in our life, we shall be free to think about what we are going to do.